Film Ireland

D1439733

Lindsay Anderson and Malcolm McDowell during the filming of *if*....

IF....

. . . .

Mark Sinker

bfi Publishing

First published in 2004 by the
BRITISH FILM INSTITUTE
21 Stephen Street, London W1P 2LN

The British Film Institute
promotes greater understanding
and appreciation of, and
access to, film and moving image
culture in the UK.

British Library Cataloguing-in-Publication Data
A catalogue record for this book is available from the British Library

ISBN 1–84457–040–1

Series design by
Andrew Barron & Collis Clements Associates

Typeset in Fournier and Franklin Gothic by
D R Bungay Associates, Burghfield, Berks

Printed in Great Britain by Cromwell Press, Trowbridge, Wiltshire

CONTENTS

ACKNOWLEDGMENTS

My early strong readers were Frank Kogan, Dr Victoria de Rijke and Ian Penman, all of whom I owe a significant debt. Thanks are also due to Norman Fay and the massed disputative minds of ilXoR, where the debate first started. And of course the inimitable surly rigour of my editor (and friend) Rob White has been exemplary.

However — in the interests of the overthrow of all critical orthodoxy — this book is lovingly dedicated to my mother and father, Margaret and Charles Sinker, who enthused about this film to me when I was still a schoolboy myself, and who taught me to laugh and to argue.

Anderson on location (with Executive Producer Roy Baird)

'IF....'

. . . .

Great schools are little societies, where a boy of any observation may see in
epitome what he will afterwards find in the world at large.

Henry Fielding

[T]hat crowd of imbeciles who find the film beautiful or poetic when it is
fundamentally a desperate and passionate call to murder.

Luis Buñuel on fans of *Un Chien andalou* (1928)

On 20 April 1999, Eric Harris and Dylan Klebold walked into Columbine
High School in Littleton, a suburb of Denver, Colorado, USA, armed
with two shotguns, a rifle and several home-made bombs. They took
hostages, executing some, sparing others – twelve classmates and a
teacher were murdered – before turning their weapons on themselves.
Luckily for many more their bombs failed to detonate.

'They were 18 and 17,' wrote my friend Frank Kogan, a Denver
resident reporting the story for the *Village Voice*,

> it was almost the end of the school year, and you look forward at the
> end of the school year to freedom. Eighteen and life: the whole vista,
> the whole landscape, is opening in front of you. They saw nothing.
> They had utterly nothing to live for and they chose to die, and there
> was no meaning in their life and they tried to give meaning to their
> death, and they came up with a really stupid meaning, a live-action
> video game with victims who really bled and couldn't fight back. A sad
> painful story, considering what must have been inside those two boys.
> However smart they were, they did not look inside themselves because
> looking at whatever was closing them off would have hurt too much.
> It hurt less to kill people and finally to kill themselves.[1]

Then Kogan took the story somewhere unusual. He got local
children talking about the world of school:

> Somehow in political discourse and in journalism, these normal
> things, normal to every high school to some degree or another –
> terror, bullying, social stratification – are not known to exist. They
> don't belong in suburbia, though every politican and reporter must
> have gone to a school, must have been in such a social stratification,

must have been in the neighborhood of terror, whether they felt it or not, whether they noticed or not. (Great line from the *Denver Post*: 'Teasing is not new.') Yet whenever these appear – terror and division – highlighted by some deadly event, they're such a surprise.[2]

At the climax of Lindsay Anderson's *if....*, five teenagers on the rooftops shoot to kill teachers, parents and fellow pupils fleeing smokebombs into a Victorian Gothic quadrangle. In December 1968, when *if....* opened – to immediate and soon prize-winning acclaim – the idea of gun crime in high schools *was* new. Writing in November 1969, in the introduction to the published screenplay, Anderson had described *if....* as 'a film dedicated to "understanding"... an incitement to *thought*'.[3] Yet in 2002, when the BFI's release of a new print of the film was handsomely publicised, the enthusiastic response played mainly to a cult consensus, the mainstream blessing the maverick long after the danger passed: 'an anarchist punk dream'; 'bristling with insolence and fomenting with revolutionary desire'; 'a bugle signalling the end of the old order'. Surely a bit too comfortably self-congratulatory – in the wake of Dunblane – for a film dedicated to understanding and thought?[4]

Of course it's fatuous to blame the Columbine terror duo's sense of injustice, rage or rebelhood on a movie they maybe never saw. Those who see themselves as outsiders may be emboldened by the fantasies they identify with, the crusades they imagine themselves undertaking; but the consciousness of exclusion is a social fact born and nurtured within schools themselves, so that – and this is Kogan's point – plenty of this same defensive-combative self-identification persists, unconsciously, *outside* and *after* the world of school. Good or bad, mainstream society values all this: it's what it secretly thinks school is for. That's how *if....* speaks to so many; as a film about a school, it circles Kogan's insight. And yet, to judge by the nostalgic comfort its fans find in it, it somehow in the end switches audience attention away from this side of the story, back into that routine generational-rebel posturing which serves present-day forces of conformity so well.

For decades the avant-garde had declared its radicalism through rhetorical calls to demolish the Academy, to torch the libraries and flood the museums. But it wasn't until the late 1960s that education *as a whole* came under attack, as the prime machinery of social conformism. 'Long live the ephemeral!' yelled the Situationists, and by 1968, popular film, music and design were being recruited into a Children's Crusade against what made the squares square – and beyond this against the Vietnam war and the killing machines of the West. Pop culture was a vector of new values against old; when these students became teachers in their turn, some tried complicatedly to accommodate within their syllabuses the populist overthrow of anything youth jibbed at. Yet *if....* remains far less dated than most films made deliberately to accord with this brief cultural convulsion.

Conception–Production–Reception
Anderson first read the screenplay, at that time called *Crusaders*, in July 1966. The earliest version dates to May 1960, a work of autobiographically specific revenge on Tonbridge school in Kent, loathed all-male alma mater of two Oxford undergraduates, David Sherwin and John Howlett. Back from the holidays, Mick and Johnny are already pining for girls. To escape the bad food, the 'nightly beatings and buggery', Mick has an affair with a younger boy, Johnny with a town girl.[5] Both are flogged and expelled: Mick runs away to sea, Johnny takes the girl to a fun-fair. Several potential producers had already hated the earlier versions.[6] Nicholas Ray – *Rebel Without a Cause* (1955) was Sherwin's and Howlett's favourite film – had liked the idea, but thought someone English should direct: Seth Holt at Ealing thought it should be a Public School man. He also knew Anderson had gone to Cheltenham College.[7]

Anderson was in a lull. His first feature, *This Sporting Life*, about a professional rugby league player willing to play foul for success, had done badly at the box office – because, Anderson proudly and unapologetically maintained, it was 'too harsh to be accepted as entertainment by the British public'.[8] The vogue for social realism in British cinema was faltering by 1963 – killed by this film, some said. But Anderson himself was by then associated with no fewer than four movements entering the downcurve of fashion.

In 1947, with school and university friend Gavin Lambert, he had started *Sequence*, an independent film quarterly. Though it never embraced Hollywood the way (for example) *Cahiers du Cinéma* would, its critical rigour – including spirited attacks on the tepidity of British film – gained it attention, and Lambert was invit-

Playing foul for success (*This Sporting Life*, Independent Artists, 1963)

ed to edit and revivify the BFI's *Sight and Sound*. Here was published Anderson's 'Only Connect', a pioneering study of documentarist Humphrey Jennings's 40s documentaries, with their 'striking associations of image, sound, music and comment ... connecting and connecting'.[9]

At London's Royal Court Theatre (RCT) in the mid-50s, Tony Richardson and actor George Devine had set up their English Stage Company to perform new drama disdained by the West End mainstream, in particular Brecht. In 1956, the play of the year – of the decade – was John Osborne's debut *Look Back in Anger*, and the Angry Young Man (AYM) movement had convulsed British theatre. Richardson, another *Sight and Sound* contributor, had invited Anderson to direct plays at the RCT in 1957, where he helped shape its austere, semi-experimental, politically committed aesthetic. The dramatists being nurtured rejected the urbane, witty drama of the 40s – notably Noël Coward's and Terence Rattigan's well-crafted entertainments – as parochial and lightweight, their stylishness as emotional concealment: in short, if the past was 'middleclass', here was the raging future.

In 1955 Richardson and Karol Reisz had co-directed a twenty-minute documentary about teddyboys and girls dancing at a jazz club, *Momma Don't Allow*. But with television buoyant, and a moribund British cinema exciting audiences as little as it had Lambert and Anderson's *Sequence*, film documentary shorts were doomed, as hard to show as see. Anderson, by then himself a documentarist in Jennings's footsteps for almost a decade, was well aware of the lack of commercial possibility. His solution – short-term but effective – was to invent his own movement and write its manifesto, complete with mini-season at the NFT, featuring

Free Cinema: 'a style means an attitude' (*Every Day Except Christmas*, Graphic Films, 1957)

Momma, his own ten-minute *O Dreamland* (named for its subject, a popular amusement park), and Lorenza Mazzetti's *Together* (set in the East End). From 1956–9, six documentary mini-seasons followed, including work by Polanski, Truffaut and Chabrol: this was 'Free Cinema' (see Appendix).

By decade's end, these three elements – the need for a new cinema, the fact of a new theatre, the fascination with working-class culture – had fused to produce a fourth, the social-realist film movement known, more cheekily than supportively, as 'Kitchen Sink'. The French New Wave had emerged from *Cahiers*'s war on critical orthodoxy: now (it was claimed) a handful of novelists, playwrights and actors – mainly Northern-born, abetted by eager directors and playgoers, mainly not – were providing the materials, the energy, the observational insight for something similar in Britain. Osborne's box-office triumph with *Anger* – the play made film – bankrolled director Tony Richardson's new production company Woodfall. Reisz directed *Saturday Night and Sunday Morning*, Richardson *The Loneliness of the Long Distance Runner*, both for Woodfall, in 1960 and 1962 respectively, making stars of Albert Finney and Tom Courtenay. Anderson had worked with both on-stage in *Billy Liar* in 1960, for the RCT. *Saturday Night* made money, allowing Reisz to produce Anderson's *This Sporting Life*.

Kitchen Sink mannerisms included double-decker rides, pints in pubs, poky tenement rooms, loud fights in accents of variable accuracy, and unhappy sex: there's more to *Life* than these, but the cultural novelty was already chewed out of them, and they muffled Anderson's subtler intentions. 'Middleclass critics – and of course all critics are middleclass, by definition – didn't really like these films,' he was still insisting in the mid-80s: '"Kitchen Sink" was the standard derisive epiphet – with the implication that they all looked the same, like wogs or chinamen …'[10] More relevant was a shift in working-class tastes and self-image, which these various intertwined movements had themselves contributed to.

In 1957's critical bestseller *The Uses of Literacy*, Richard Hoggart had mourned the lost community values of the Northern back-to-backs, swept away by teenage fads from America: jukeboxes, milkbars, jazz. In 'Get Out and Push', an essay published in *Declaration*, an AYM manifesto, Anderson was still denouncing the British movie as 'emotionally inhibited, wilfully blind to the conditions and problems of the present':[11] the nation was coddled and cocooned in an infant's nursery, alarming noises off ignored. Free Cinema was his first antidote – yet the documentary form seemed to project a passivity onto its subjects, the downtrodden viewed in their own habitat, a voiceover explaining to you (by definition middle-class) all you saw. *O Dreamland* had just such a narration, but consider now lines from the two manifestos: 'The image speaks ... Sound amplifies and comments ... A style means an attitude ... You can use your eyes and ears ... You can give indications.' The voice stays neutral; it's the interweave of juxtapositions which implies this shoddy carnival is just a prison for working-class dreams. The form twists against observer class-complacency: but still the anger may feel patronising, ventriloquised on behalf of the culturally torpid.

Nevertheless the AYM movement, this contradictory and limited fashionable snarl, was a breakthrough moment, as a rising generation stepped forward as auteurs of their own unflinching authenticity, playing themselves – or people very like – on-stage or in print. And their immediate successors – led by The Beatles, four lads from Northern back-to-backs – sparked a cultural revolt which swamped Hoggart's sulk. American-style glamour and flight called, and the middle-class fascination with British working-class culture, this core of non-effete honesty, foundered. *A Hard Day's Night* (1964) is really the film that killed Kitchen Sink. Yet Anderson – who openly detested Richard Lester's mannerist shallowness, and was ever unpersuaded by the recondite Godard – was nevertheless the only Free Cineaste to intuit the scale of the rupture imported from Memphis via Liverpool, and to respond.

His next film project, begun in 1965 and rarely seen today, was a movie short, *The White Bus*, scripted by Shelagh Delaney from her own short story.[12] Salford-born, Delaney was also reacting against Rattigan and Coward – her stage play *A Taste of Honey* became Richardson's own

Dummy armageddon (*The White Bus*, Holly Productions, 1966)

Kitchen Sink movie – but she was younger than the AYM-ists, her low-key pop-modernism quite different from their tantrum-rich noisiness. An office girl takes a train home to, then a tourist bus round Salford, where Arthur Lowe's lecherous mayor expands on the sights: industrial estates, housing estates, libraries, arts centres. Black and white with momentary colour splashes, *Bus* is gently, impatiently sardonic about provincial, self-satisfied England, that thinks itself so progressive. A training exercise against atomic attack collapses into Python-prescient fantasy: the girl walks from dummy Armageddon back into her wary, bohemian margin.

Anderson's earliest documentaries had observed with approval lively communities not his own: via *Life* and *Bus*, he was now developing a kind of vicarious disenchantment. Did he see in *Crusaders* his own *White Bus*: a return to his own public school roots – to revisit the terror, the division, to capture it, blow it all up, walk quietly away? If Cowardist emotional concealment was the enemy, didn't AYM-ist orthodoxy now require Anderson be open about the world that made *him*? But going home can be hard.

Before leaving for Warsaw, where he was directing an Osborne play and making a documentary, Anderson had ordered Sherwin and Howlett to take *Crusaders* – which he thought a sentimental, adolescent mess – to pieces. In November 1966 he wrote to Sherwin: 'I haven't mentioned, and am not sure if I should, what is the *theme* of this film.' We recognise the characters mentioned in this letter, but not the plotlines. Does Anderson know what he wanted yet? He seems to be sounding his own unconscious as much as Sherwin's, trusting – as he always did – in intuition: 'What is necessary now is to be CONCRETE. The TRUTH is always interesting.'[13]

1967 saw Holt and Howlett leaving, unhappy with the script's direction. Sherwin and Anderson continued alone, 'with no thought of pleasing anyone but ourselves'.[14] From mid-March, at Anderson's Sussex cottage, they worked on it almost every day. An outline for a scene would be agreed: Sherwin wrote it, Anderson commented, Sherwin rewrote. Sherwin did the dialogue, but needed Anderson to help develop ideas for scenes. All the while they swapped memories of their respective times in respective schools. By mid-May 1967, they had a draft they liked.

No major film company did. In June, hawking the idea down Wardour Street itself, Anderson met Albert Finney, flush with the international success of *Tom Jones* and just completing his first film (*Charlie Bubbles*, from a script by Delaney) for his own production company, Memorial Enterprises. Finney's business partner, Michael Medwin, agreed to co-produce: Charles Bludhorn, at Paramount in New

York, was married to a Finney fan, and got his people to greenlight the script without even reading it. Paramount UK, pretending they hadn't either, now got behind it. The budget was to be a quarter of a million pounds – austere but not impossible.[15] Casting agent Miriam Brickman put ads in the *Times*, *Telegraph* and *Melody Maker*: thousands of potential teen-male stars would respond unsuccessfully.

Anderson hoped to shoot it at Cheltenham, and carefully bowdlerised the script he sent headmaster David Ashcroft – but was the title *Crusaders* itself a red rag? Better something 'very old-fashioned, corny and patriotic' (Anderson's phrase);[16] thinking Kipling, Medwin's secretary Daphne Hunter suggested 'If ' – to which Anderson added four ellipsis dots. In August Ashcroft gave permission. Location shooting at Cheltenham started in March 1968, and a unit of eighty-five people travelled up.

What follows is built from anecdotes and guesswork. Others have written their own accounts of how the film got made, or been interviewed – but Anderson's reticence and love for teacherly mindgames ensure his version may never properly be known.[17] Sherwin, in the often very funny *Going Mad in Hollywood – and Life with Lindsay Anderson*, writes as someone whose very being was changed, by an irresistible man he never quite understood. David Robinson wrote two on-set reports, one for the *Times*, one for *Sight and Sound*: these concentrate on Anderson's dealings with actors and – as important – non-actors, the boys and staff of Cheltenham College, the people of the town itself. Robinson describes a director in absolute control, knowing now exactly what he wants. If Anderson was sometimes snappy and impatient with these non-professionals – such as young Rupert Webster, who played pretty boy Bobby Philips – they tolerated it, and seemed to respect him.[18]

The film's editor David Gladwell's article, an introduction to what his job entails written for *Screen* the following year, tells a similar story, of a director insisting on absolute control, 'to an extent which has made it a very unconventional picture to work on'. The shooting style is old-fashioned: very precise but unobtrusive camera setups, camera movement carefully rehearsed, executed, controlled, almost no difference between takes. To Gladwell it nevertheless seemed 'as personal, if you like, as a home movie'.[19] Anderson himself, talking to Robinson, said that its 'simple shooting style' got at 'essences rather than brilliant surfaces'. To him, *if....* was a 'deliberate contravention of fashion ... a film that from the commercial point of view was regarded as outlandish and utterly uncommercial'.[20]

In Vietnam in May 1968, a Third World army turned the tide against technocratic imperialism: the Tet offensive. On campuses west and east, student uprisings. Martin Luther King and Bobby Kennedy assassinated. With uncanny editorial timing, *Sight and Sound* ran Robinson's set report on *if....* in their May issue – alongside Godard's debates with 'revolutionary' students at Berkeley on the role of the film-maker, the story of the walkout at Cannes (organised by Godard), protesting French government treatment of state film archivist Henri Langlois, and reviews of *The Graduate*, *Petulia*, *Planet of the Apes*, *2001: A Space Odyssey* and *Week-end*.

With summer turbulent everywhere, Anderson, Gladwell and others spent four or five concentrated months editing, cutting and dubbing, bringing the twenty reels of footage, an unusually spare 200 minutes, down to the final 111. Meanwhile the very events that made *if....* so timely were putting the wind up Paramount. The film screened to acclaim at the London Film Festival late in the year, then fell into a hole. But Vadim's *Barbarella*, its flip sexpop content now suddenly dated, was doing badly, Paramount had to fulfil their Eady quota for the year, and *if....* was slipped into the Plaza in December.[21] Was commercial viability the worry, or was it the political controversy that success might bring? The times became the judge: on word of mouth alone, *if....* became a runaway London hit.

Now came the prizes: at Cannes in 1969 the Palme D'Or; for Sherwin the British Writers' Guild Award for best original screenplay; for Anderson, 'Director of the Year' from *TV Mail* and *International Film Guide*. 'Which side will *you* be on?' jabbed the posters. If the archives are a guide, the answer was all but unanimous. Reviewers, lowbrow and highbrow, flocked to recommend it.

Almost alone, Eric Rhode at the *Listener* demurred, calling it 'the most hating film I know of', and 'so nightmarish and humourless that it becomes risible, a picture so unreal that it should play into the hands of the public school lobby', the final scene being 'as clear an embodiment of homosexual violence as you could wish'.[22] And with brilliant contrarian precision, Pauline Kael at the *New Yorker* attacked Anderson for the film's sudden congruence with fashionably youth-centric film-industry posture. Against all expectation, 1968's cultural *bouleversements* had made *if....* trendy: Kael used this to worm into its flaws. Anderson often used pre-release publicity as a teacherly nudge towards the correct reading. Kael, who believed the film should be doing the manipulation, not the press releases, used his political moralism against him: 'He's a scourge, not a poet, and the picture is clogged by all the difficult, ambitious things he attempts and flubs ... [We] don't really know – immediately and intuitively – why he is showing us what he is showing us.' Unlike Vigo's *Zéro de conduite* (1933), which several reviewers cited as its precursor, Anderson fatally confused the child's perspective with the radical's, she argued: a very 60s delusion, if so. Vigo's had been a liberating comic metaphor: 'the school is a *child's* mirror of society.' Anderson's idea of 'destroying the prison is to kill the inmates'.[23]

Gavin Millar – who liked a great deal its tenderness, its exactness of observation, the very surrealism that Kael felt didn't fly – picked at the same scab in his review for *Sight and Sound*: 'Are we part of the sheepish congregation whom Anderson's youthful cohorts will mow down ... [or] the gullible young, misled by that unholy alliance of jingoism and commercialism ...?' For all its qualities, the politics in *if....* – of class *and* sex – are confused, the film a vision blurred: 'Perhaps we're up on the roof behind the gatling? In that case, we want to know what kind of new society it is that we're fighting for.'[24]

A BFI Classic

'We constantly thought of Brecht,' says Anderson of the making.[25] Brecht's dramas are designed to allow the audience to sidestep the flow of unthinking identification, to coax them into analysing what's happening and why – and so this book must do the same, freezing Anderson's ideas and images to target and penetrate, like Travis in his study, firing blood-red darts at the gorgeous and the great, at popes and pin-ups. The unexamined complexities that frustrated Kael must be freed, in scene-by-scene readings of key shots, gestures, exchanges, every element linked to wider histories, political, literary, architectural, musical, and to all Anderson's oft-declared forebears: Jennings, Vigo, Ford, Buñuel ...

Recalling the miseries of their own schooldays, comfortable audiences cheer five demented teenage spree-killers: with thirty-five years' hindsight, *if....* can easily seem muddled, even reactionary. But it's important that we don't simply switch from a superficial and trendily excited approval to a superficial or a jaded hostility. Anderson looked at the world with cold fury *and* tenderness, and it's the ambiguity of this mix – of violence and reserve, temper and fondness, percipience and prejudice, the openness of a man so often scornfully didactic – which is worth exploring. This is a film which can be read – against conscious intention? – for its critique as well as its its celebration of the currents and impulses coursing through the cultural uprisings of the 60s. Anderson's attitude to his material was self-evidently complex, often contradictory: but whose isn't, when the topic is their own youth, and the times and forces which formed them?

🔔 🔔 🔔

The Book of the Film of the Book of the ...

Gordon Parry's movie of *Tom Brown's Schooldays*, a generally weak 1951 re-entry into Thomas Hughes's 1857 novel, begins with school fiction, legend and history – a hymn sung in Latin, night shots of the cloisters and empty quadrangle of Rugby School – in such condensed reference that the story itself (bullying, fightback, earnest moral) feels shadowed by a dream. *if....*, beginning no less compactly, follows a biblical epigraph with a bleached, tinted still of Cheltenham College, the school song fading into ambient boy-tumult, and the title: 'if ' in lower case, plus dots. By the time Anderson's own name appears, beginning the extended credits, the soundtrack has changed. Composer Marc Wilkinson studied under Edgard Varèse, and we enter that vein here: modernist, hard to parse, as spikily unsettled as a Calder mobile. And now the first chapter heading: '1. College House – Return'. (There are eight chapters in all.)

The biblical quotation – 'Wisdom is the principle thing; therefore get wisdom: and with all thy getting, get understanding' – nudges us to receive everything condensed into this preface as evidence in a case not yet stated: image, music, text, the speech lurking in the schoolboy din, itself an echo of *Zéro de conduite*.[26] Compared with Godard's gnomic primary-colour flatness or Lester's proto-music-video rush, the opening feels measured, bookish, un-60s. The invocation of Kipling's best-loved poem may already remind some of us of his subversive trio of pupils, from his 1899 collection *Stalky and Co*, a key precursor:

A tumult of boys, echoing Vigo's *Zéro de conduite* (Argui-Film, 1933)

Boys that [the Housemaster] understood attended House-matches and could be accounted for at any moment. But he had heard M'Turk openly deride cricket – even House-matches; Beetle's views on the honour of the House he knew were incendiary; and he could never tell when the soft and smiling Stalky was laughing at him.[27]

As a school story, *Stalky* wages endless serpentine war with the moralising orthodoxies of its predecessor *Tom Brown*. And if you know this, won't the poem's counterfactual recipe for manliness – 'If you can meet with Triumph and Disaster, and treat those two imposters just the same' – feel more dissident than corny?[28] Connecting and connecting, yes, just like a Jennings documentary – there are several layers of revisionary rewrite, in several media, deftly packed in here – but perhaps we're swept past some of them before we quite *can* connect.

Trunks, Owners, Corridors
A boy drops a can of beans, and two others instantly clatter it away down the hall with their hockey sticks as he swears: the first scene is fun and funny, uplifting even – genuine kid's stuff, well caught on camera. Editor David Gladwell loved the handling of the first ten shots of the film: 'Many times we would return to the sequence to try something fresh and each time, I think, we improved it.'[29] The exposition – all camerawork and tight cuts – throws viewers into the grabby bustle of documentary, and holds us. Social hierarchy will be established with extraordinary subliminal economy in this chapter: show not tell.

In his essay 'Democratising the Intellect', Frank Kogan explores the making of the modern mind:

and I say that school tries to enforce a split between classroom and hallway. The split tells us that to be intellectual we have to live in the classroom and to obey the classroom rule, which is to talk not to and about other people but just about some third thing, 'the subject matter'. It says that to talk to and about each other, as we do in the hallways, isn't to think but to merely live our lives. And so – the split claims – either we can use our intellect or we can live our lives, but we can't do both at once. And living our lives (as the hallways narrowly construes this) becomes 'visceral' by default, since our lives have been ejected from the 'intellect'. And the hallway's vengeance on the classroom is to say, 'You may be smart, but I'm *real* and you're not.' But this is an impoverished realness, since it expels anything that the classroom defines as 'mental', and forbids our putting something off in the distance and reflecting on it.[30]

All school tales play the inherited lore of the corridor against the approved language of the classroom – because in all real schools, we learn many different codes of expression and interaction and understanding in each zone, and they jostle against one another, laughing or swearing. But only *if...* was made in a season when the established system of approved classroom knowledge was under such freewheeling self-attack. In 1968, the pull of film – away from the literary and story-borne to the combined rival energies of sound and image – had also become a jostle of new, non-classroom codes.

The Tenth Shot
In the canonic British school story, we are inducted into an unfamiliar world via the journey of a guileless innocent: here one Jute at the school noticeboard, newest of the new, lowest of the low, like Sade's Justine busily quizzing all the wrong people.

In 1957, during a *Cahiers* round-table on the state of French cinema, someone asked about the mediocrity of *British* cinema, and Jacques Rivette explained: 'British cinema is a genre cinema, but one where the genres have no genuine roots.'[31] Jump nearly four decades, to *Typically British*, a BFI television history made and narrated by UK director Stephen Frears, who was 'Assistant to the Director' on *if....* Frears first quotes Truffaut on the incompatibility between the term 'cinema' and Britain, then – with a robust 'Bollocks to Truffaut!' – jumps into a sequence of caning clips from British movies: *Goodbye, Mr. Chips* (1939); *Housemaster* (1938); *The Guinea Pig* (1948), followed by Will Hay's *Boys Will Be Boys* (1935) – which Anderson adored – and *if....* itself.[32]

From new boy's quest to head boy's command: Jute and Rowntree

The boarding school story *is* a British genre, with genuine roots: central to the Romance of Empire, its history as a genre – both literary and otherwise – is a map of the fortunes of Empire, from mid-life crisis to zenith to dismantlement. Hughes's *Brown* and Dean Farrar's *Eric, or Little by Little* (1858) were the hits which established it – arriving as the imperial project wobbled in the wake of Crimea and the Indian Mutiny. These two authors shared a faith in the 'manliness' of Christ, as the model for moral reform across the globe. A torrent of boys' magazines and books followed, the formula streamlined through the 1880s till it ran as smoothly as the colonies. In 1899, with *Stalky*, Kipling added layers of mocking darkness, exploring the links between the propagation of knowledge and the policing of Empire. After World War 1, with the colonies increasingly recalcitrant, the genre dodged fraught *Stalky*-style experiment for Billy Bunter-type comfort food. As the long imperial retreat sounded in the 50s, a hitherto unBritish scepticism towards hierarchy declared itself: the kids that flow in clouds across bomb-scarred London in *Hue and Cry* (1946) are channelling Vigo's class warfare in *Zéro* towards the delirious, summer

The British and French school canons (clockwise from top left): *Tom Brown's School Days* (George Minter Productions, 1951); Will Hay in *Boys Will Be Boys* (Gainsborough Pictures, 1935); *Les Quatre cents coups* (Films du Carrosse, 1959); *Zéro de conduite*

anarchisms of *The Happiest Days of Your Life* (1950) and the *St Trinians* no-go zone (1954–66), all energy contained and revealed in the mass.

Kid-centred fiction grounds itself on the selected, the mythologised, the hidden – long-ago traumas transfigured into legend, to cope with the now. In cinema's childhood, children mainly still functioned as plot-driving Victorian icons of pathos; in the decades between the world wars, youth, not a constant but a concept with a history, vanished almost entirely from the screen; from the 50s, it would grow to become the main subject (and market) for Hollywood. In France, Vigo's spawn mastered cameras. Godard's 1959 *Cahiers* review of Truffaut's film about himself as a schoolboy is a compact 300-word paragraph breaking up in a machine-gun jabber of nouns: 'To sum up, what shall I say? This: *Les 400 coups* will be a film signed Frankness. Rapidity. Art. Novelty. Cinematograph. Originality. Impertinence. Seriousness. Tragedy. Renovation. Ubu-Roi. Fantasy. Ferocity. Affection. Universality. Tenderness.'[33] The new pop cinema treats the young as confused but honourably feisty harbingers of a better future, teen sex and generation gap as motor and weapon respectively, the inability to grow up a blueprint for all social criticism and individualism, germ of the Children's Crusade of the late 60s.[34]

By contrast here at the start of *if....*, to survive is to know your place, to lose individuality along with innocence. A small, moon-faced newcomer *may* be manly head boy one day – except what do *we* mean by 'manly'?

'Scum!'

With a beautiful shout, Robert Swann's head boy Rowntree empties the hallway. Where the press of boy traffic fills these narrow spaces without owning them, Rowntree commands space, theirs and his own. He has style and charisma: such is his authority that we may have missed the disconnected topsyturviness of his earlier command, here repeated: 'Run! *Run* in the corridor!'

When the 'Scum Call' rings out, the wretched of this earth must fly to its bidding, as little Jute has the wit to guess. In all canonic (male) school stories, fagging is a key social fact: in return for his servitude, the fag receives physical protection and help with schoolwork from the seniors he fags for. 'The little boys,' wrote the flabbergasted Parisian journalist Hippolyte Taine in the late 1860s, 'are valets and slaves' – his reports were based on Eton, Harrow and *Tom Brown*.[35]

There's more: after the crackle of hallway conflict, the first throb of attraction. Rowntree is amusedly avuncular with – and interested in –

Jute. Is this interest mutual? If Jute the boy does one day become Rowntree the man, will he use fags as slaves? The film's slang – 'scum', 'bumf-tutor' – is invented: it *sounds* obscure and exclusionary, but is of course perfectly comprehensible, its class-bound sexual undercurrents only too clear.

Sweat Room

Brunning shows Jute the space where juniors pass their non-sleeping lives. Self-expression is limited to locker space for books, magazines, pin-ups, non-perishable food; privacy all but imaginary; intimacy communal. The juniors have a tolerated measure of self-ownership, but it's a camaraderie punctuated – cemented – by the scuffles of a rough democracy: Machin (Richard Davis) is jeered when he reminds them of Sweat Room rules. On the walls, we glimpse a sparse countercultural iconography: Che, Geronimo, Alan Aldridge's cover design for *The Penguin Book of Comics*.

Tarting

Rupert Webster's Bobby Philips knows he's pretty: a junior he may be, but he can barter with his attractiveness a degree of control over his space. When others gather to leer, they're driven off by Hugh Thomas's prefect Denson, paying court his own way: 'Philips, stop tarting ... you need a haircut.' We've not yet been told that prefects are called 'Whips' in this place, but nevertheless the scene swiftly establishes the complexity of this pecking order, its jigsaw of official with sexual and other, harder-to-define power structures. Self-hatingly held by Philips's allure, Denson protects the younger boy from harassment, but his petty tyranny and

Enter Travis, masked

hypocrisy render his boss Rowntree's self-possession all the more charismatic. Enter now a vigorous figure carrying a trunk, head swathed in hat and scarf, position on the social staircase excitingly mysterious to us. Masked as he is, sartorially and in manner, Malcolm McDowell's Mick Travis commands stairs *and* screen, as fully as anyone we've seen. He hustles up the stairs past Denson, will later bump into him on the way down: battle for dominion is joined.

A Secret Moustache

Hat and scarf still in place in the dormitory, refusing to respect the sumptuary laws of the school's intimate spaces, Travis spars with mid-level authority: Stephans (Guy Ross). Later, in his dingy study, alone with Munch's *The Scream* and a Mao poster, Travis clips his Beatles-style Edwardian moustache one last loving time before shaving it off. Only Knightly (David Wood) can be trusted to view it, which he does, grinning admiringly: 'God, you're ugly – you look evil.'

'Yes,' replies Travis. 'My face is a never-ending source of wonder to me.'

In his hostile review, Eric Rhode was confused: 'Many of the boys do not resemble public school types, and ... the actor playing Mick looks and behaves as though he came from a remand school.'[36] Anderson had been very drawn to the un-'actorish' young actors moving from the hinterlands into West End theatre, free from the 'curse of middle-class inhibitions'[37] – though jolt-of-realness had become shtick in its turn: McDowell was from Liverpool, but his model is surely Mick Jagger, whose London-suburban, game-playing persona was everywhere in the

On looking evil

late 60s, a prancingly difficult class-fluid threat, all performative self-awareness and brilliantly unsettling and theatrical-manipulative use of same. David Hemmings had been Jagger's first screen stand-in: across a blur of genres, McDowell took the same mix far further: arrogance, insolence, swagger, camp, cruelty, sensual near-ugliness, intensely sexy dislikeability, a *faux*-childlike mask of non-innocent innocence, the genuine menace of the destructive thug archetype as (hugely popular) fantasy come-on. Not even noticing a distant Scum Call – *they're* not scum – Knightly and Travis swap unlikely tales of holiday exploits.

Masters with Whips
The dining room is spacious, walled with portraits of masters past, but it's the prefects – sweeping in unobstructed, embroidered waistcoats, bullyboy canes, magnificent in their eighteenth-century arrogance – who make it an extension of their disciplinary gaze. Dowdy and ineffectual by comparison, the housemaster, Arthur Lowe's Mr Kemp, encourages newcomers: soon they'll find their way around. Translation: soon they'll learn that the Whips are the only masters here. As Hughes, Taine and Kipling all hint, this upside-down order thrived because so effective once out in the world.[38]

As a pragmatic pedagogic approach to the devolution of power and responsibility, it had been discovered in India: non-conformists Joseph Lancaster and Andrew Bell imported into Britain in the 1790s the so-called 'Madras System', in which older boys passed what they'd been taught down to younger, in schoolroom production-line cascade-chain. The wild eighteenth century had in fact very nearly seen off the English Public

Disciplinary gaze: the Whips

School (EPS): schoolmasters were the mere hirelings of the sons of the gentry, and pupil power held sway as intake fell drastically – at Shrewsbury, headmaster James Atcherly spent his time competing with his twenty or so boys to kick high a bacon flitch hung from the kitchen ceiling. Atcherly's successor, the reforming headmaster Samuel Butler, revived and Madras-ised the prefect system, to allow an overworked staff to focus on matters academic. In return for official privileges of dress and behaviour, a small cadre of trusted senior boys administered respect for the teachers – and themselves.

Butler's method ballooned out into the entire nineteenth-century educational system, via the revitalised EPS. As the decades passed and numbers revived, the Madras System also proved ideal for the management, by a scattering of manly types, of the half-sullen millions of Empire. Coaxing a screenplay out of Sherwin, Anderson would describe the EPS as 'a strange sub-world, with its own peculiar laws, distortions, brutalities, loves [and] its special relationship to a perhaps outdated conception of British society'.[39] If they leavened fagging with a legacy of patriarchal responsibility, the seniors had seen that this sub-world could sustain itself over time. Its longevity demanded the creation of a committed, close-knit, self-replicating microclass of Empire-builders, soldiers and administrators. If ritual and tradition are all the knowledge you'll need here, learning and discipline become the same thing. Academic teachers were a pretext; system-loyal Whips were what mattered.

The camaraderie of the trio is a rebuke to all this, in and out of character. Writing to Lowe's son Stephen, David Wood recalled the making of this scene:

> Your father's performance, from the very first rehearsal, was so funny, not in an overt way, but in its reality and sincerity. I remember that Malcolm McDowell, Richard Warwick and I were all standing listening by a table near the front. We started corpsing, unable to contain our laughter at your father's performance. It really was splendidly funny. Lindsay Anderson became very annoyed with us for interrupting the scene, and after several repeat performances of uncontrollable giggling, we were kicked out of the hall and threatened with loss of our reaction close-ups![40]

Indeed, the *fore*ground story here – Wallace (Richard Warwick) shoving others aside to join Knightly and Travis – is a bit perfunctory.

Surely the three-man revolutionary army will have been trusted compadres before the story even starts?

Bedroom Manners †[41]
The untrammelled Jagger-thug briefly presents as *bien-pensant* standard bearer, when Travis silences the anti-Semitic Stephans. Authority – via Rowntree's mastery of the space, as he enters with his posse to inspect – will be formally handed back to Stephans. It's stripped from him the moment the Whips leave, when the trio applaud, first mockingly, then menacingly.

Authority is also a matter of timing. During the health inspection, there's the Whips' brisk time-saving juxtaposition: 'Heath certificate? Ringworm? Eye disease? VD? Confirmation class?' Later they stalk the corridors shouting 'Dormitory Inspection in Three Minutes!' in exact unsignalled unison – the exactness marking an unchallenged will-to-choreograph ('Lights out!' is followed by a unison blackout). But Travis has this gift too, amusing himself by doffing his dressing gown in a single fluid movement, a lovely, funny trick we'll see again – then bounding, again in one move at naughty last minute, into bed, a rogue alpha male's impish style trumping Stephans' bad imitation.

In among these all-male dormitory scenes, we watch Mrs Kemp (Mary MacLeod) lead the new teacher (Ben Aris) upstairs to his garret. Compared even to the utilitarian shittiness of the studies – so set-designed grimy brown they're comical – this room seems desolate, lonely and mean, doubly so with the film stock switching to sudden meagre monochrome. Sexual hunger emanates from Mrs Kemp: despite the hidden dirty joke of his name, teacher John Thomas doesn't respond – does he even notice?

In the junior dorm, Jute's knees – tenting up the bedclothes when all others sit flat – mark him as a hold-out uncaptured mote still, his posture as incorrect as his diary (which belongs in the Sweat Room, with all 'privacy').

This film is a dense map of establishment systems of power in the world, and the transmissions of official knowledge, discipline, law. But it contrasts these with rival systems of power and understanding, individual relationships as dance of repulsion and attraction, conflict and desire. The rituals of boy world as mobile *mise en scène*: rituals of sex and violence in particular, the rank and file reinforcing the pecking order with every exchange, from baked-bean hockey to seniors stroking your hair. Establishment wisdom is complicit with all these also; and blind to them, and vulnerable.

🪔 🪔 🪔

Morning Sun

Anderson often said he had no visual sense: his faithful sidekick Jocelyn Herbert – with him since the late 50s at the Royal Court Theatre (RCT), though this was her first film as designer – had famously declared her intention to remove the clutter from stage decoration. But clutter is just what you can't quite remove from films shot documentary-style, and this second chapter provides the first exteriors.

No official architecture was ever more flamboyantly theatrical than Victorian Gothic. Once an avant-garde fashion – disdaining eighteenth-century neo-classical orthodoxy by dressing up as a wild imaginary past – the Gothic revival went respectable in the 1830s, supplying the replacement when Parliament burned down. Such was the confidence of the reforming establishment that this compromise blur of invented traditions was chosen as the backdrop of the heart of Empire. As the middle classes played at being the aristocrats they were ousting, behind them soared this practical, crabbed, energetic monumentality, its civilising mission world-historical, unique – barbarian *and* imperial, chaotic *and* orderly, organic *and* mathematical. Its very unclarity was central to its success: somehow it combined Anglo-Saxon liberty, Norman toughness, Tudor boldness, secret Catholic worldliness, public Puritan uplift ... Outside and within, Cheltenham College – founded as a school in 1841, its postcard-pastiche chapel built in the 1890s – puts us in unconscious mind of *whichever element we need* from this magnificently unstable imperial oneness.

Chapel within†

John Ruskin, Tory communist, passionate aesthete, possible virgin, the leading dissident Victorian intellectual, had hailed medieval cathedral Gothic as an explicitly *social* form, with its lively gargoyle detail courtesy of anonymous carver-workmen locked into a joyful teamwork under a

Establishment shots: Cheltenham College in *if ....*; Repton in *Goodbye, Mr. Chips* (Metro-Goldwyn-Mayer British Studios, 1939)

master architect's eye, individual freedom grounded in history and humane tradition. And it's the sense of community here, visual and aural, which allows these camera studies of individuals – here eager, there nervily frantic – to achieve their swift living precision. Some are out of place in their carved pews, bored with the show: but while the unimpressed have superficial camera approval, the soundtrack cherishes the sad, solemn, comforting power of massed masculine *ordinary* singing voices.

Headmaster

The first exterior proper shows the reach of the headmaster's domain, pointed windows, multicoloured bricks, balconies, archways and jagged spires, as evocative a backdrop as Ford's Monument Valley, the entire school his stage, as he struts, juggling all-comers, never listening. A music-hall caricature, complained some reviewers – but Peter Jeffrey's performance is a comic joy throughout, perfectly written, perfectly executed. Besides, headmasters in this tradition act as deliberate cartoons of themselves – first because children respond to it, second because tradition invoked is both continued justification and justification-by-continuity. Just as the history of theatre is a grand pantheon of actors – Garrick, Keane, Gielgud, Olivier – the Heroic Age of the EPS is a procession of great names, a grand pantheon of Doctors: Butler of Shrewsbury, pioneer of EPS reform; Arnold of Rugby, avatar of Victorian Establishment morality; the brilliant, terrible Keate of Eton, revered for birching eighty boys in a single day in 1832.

The entire school his stage

Brownian Motion

Boys tussle through a cloister, the energy easily contained and directed by these weathered stone lanes, these ancient arteries. It's a choreography Anderson and Sherwin have totally internalised. Anderson – former senior prefect himself at Cheltenham – knows in his bones how to induce this behaviour in his gambolling non-actors.

How Not to Learn History

Drab and brown as the room, Graham Crowden's unnamed teacher's shabbiness is a vestigial protest against the wing-collar dandyism of school uniform. He's quite mad, riding his bike into the room loudly singing the 'Pilgrim' hymn we just heard in chapel, throwing windows wide, tossing essays about without care or grace. Unmoved, the class watches a jaded adult amusing only himself: this could be a conventional school comedy, unthreatening as the japes in the Molesworth books – yet in the details, fleeting traces of response, vulnerability, hope, despair, are telling strikes against the pretensions of the college.

The first lesson of the first day of term; his face searching theirs for a gleam of response as he asks a question; he's ravenous for connection. Getting none, he switches off again, reads a paper while they write: if the scene is emblematic of futility at the grand level – so much for knowledge, wisdom, understanding – it's also emblematic, at the (human, detailed) level, of a complex mutual betrayal. This teacher's intellect is as meaningless to rebels as to conformists (Whip Denson is the butt of teacherly scorn). Travis is clearly a favourite, and flickering at the edge of their exchange is a road not taken, his essay lost 'somewhere in the Mont Blanc tunnel', the teacher assuming it was good. Travis grins, but doesn't his expression then move on, just for a second, beyond chosen pose and into exasperation, even hurt? Can we build with any certainty on so momentary a glimpse of hidden feelings? If one unnamed teacher's carelessness can be a betrayal, was the possibility for communication, let alone alliance, always just a chimera?

(By contrast Kipling allowed his antiheroes in *Stalky* to dislike and disoblige unpleasant teachers: but they never were *bad* teachers, nor did he ever imply their subjects were worthless. Be the means never so contrary, Kipling insisted, something of value was being seeded in these mocking, wilful heads.)

His class still unmoved, this teacher sighs and sets them an essay based on a quotation: 'It has been said that King George III was a mollusc who never found his rock.' One last try: 'Said by whom, Travis?' Travis beams, as serenely innocent and insolent as only McDowell can be: 'Plumb? J. H. Plumb?' Teacher (expression unreadable): 'Po-o-ossibly.' If it's a guess, it's a creditable guess: Plumb was a leading scholar of eighteenth-century history. It may be a bluff; Travis may be right, catching the teacher in his own trap – but whichever it is, it constitutes *Travis's* refusal to connect, to acknowledge a perceptive irony; his betrayal-in-return.

A detail: given the impenetrability of the original question the teacher asks his class, its significance emerges only if we hold it still and think:

> In studying the nineteenth century, one thing will be clear – that the growth of technology (telegraph, cheap newspapers, railways, transport) is matched by a failure of imagination ... a fatal inability to understand the meaning and consequences of all these levers, wires and railways – climaxing in 1914 when the German Kaiser is told by his generals that he can't stop the war he has started because it will spoil the railway timetables on which victory depended. Or perhaps you fashionably and happily believe that it's all a matter of evil dictators, rather than whole populations of evil people like ... ourselves? Do you disagree? Don't you find this version of history facile? Do you have a view?

A jaded adult, amusing only himself, tosses essays about, while the pupil plays the teacher's games back at him

Left hanging, this matter of 'fatal inability' swells to engulf the apparent morality of the entire narrative – and the cleansing war that none have the wit to stop. College stands for 'excellence in television and the entertainment industries,' the headmaster will shortly tell the Whips, smugly. But not even the revolutionaries yet see how the modern camera eye is about to shatter this quasi-medieval social ecology: is this Anderson's facile evasion, or his deep point? (Do you have a view?)

Disfigured Gothic

Through an elaborate multi-arched window, we can see floor levels altered since construction: the window now serves classrooms on two floors. Shoddy current architecture has usurped well-made Victorian homage to social harmony: thus the workings of this school, clumsily at odds with its historical and cultural pretensions. Inside, teaching the juniors by rote, Geoffrey Chater's chaplain stalks this ugly attic of a room; the geometry the camera makes of his movements – especially compared with the seeming indifference of his historian colleague – is sinister and perverse, till questions about angles turn sadistic opportunities: he clouts Brunning from behind and tweaks a nipple inside Jute's shirt. This character was apparently based on someone from Anderson's Cheltenham[42] – but such insider knowledge is misleading: to have force, the film requires this corruptly avuncular figure to be morally general rather than autobiographically particular, to be a type not an anomaly.

'You Could Say We Were Middleclass'

When the Victorians said 'Public School', their model was the Nine 'Great Public Schools': Winchester, Eton, St Paul's, Shrewsbury, Rugby, Harrow, Westminster, Charterhouse and Merchant Taylors, each with centuries of grand tradition behind them. We're meant to think this too,

Questions about angles turn sadistic opportunities: the chaplain and Jute

as the headmaster so glibly outlines the purpose of College to the Whips, complete with daring 'sexy' joke. It's a parody of present-day values, of tradition corrupted by commerce.

Except the EPS has *always been middle class*. Even Eton was founded by merchants, during the Wars of the Roses. Most of the Nine were in effect a bribe, the Tudor dynasty undermining the landed barons by buying the loyalties of the rising bourgeoisie with grandiose educational foundations. If this system fell into disrepair after the Civil War, the 1840s, the Great Age of Victorian Reform, saw a rash of copycat schools – Marlborough, Haileybury, Oundle, Cheltenham, scores more – exploiting a vast new market, the purchase of a superior learning promised and delivered. Reluctantly even the Nine were pressured to conform to the practice of their uppity imitators: exams, marks for work, prize-giving on speechdays – when schoolchums past, generals and archbishops now, were being paraded to woo the parents of pupils future, commercial draw disguised as ancient timeless continuity, the paying customer lured by marriage of scholarship with salesmanship. After Butler's genuine scholarly idealism, the reactionary utopia of meritocracy.

Peter Jeffrey's headmaster is a slick pragmatist, his values neatly dissected: he's never heard of the composer Buxtehude, and drama isn't even noise to him; he teaches Business Studies. But our speed-read judgment will not be formed by contrasting him with his historical forebears, because the canonic school story since *Tom Brown* has conspired with the generic EPS prospectus to occlude any useable social history – which is to say, true self-knowledge – of schools. In the British bourgeois utopia, aristocrat is mimicked by meritocrat. Thus did the middle classes liquidate their precursors: by imitation.

Language Lab
The specialist slang Jute is being brutally taught is openly class- and gender-biased, parodically hostile to outsiders: 'town girls: *Town Tarts*; grammar school: *Smudges*; all others: *Bloody Oiks...*' This is obligatory knowledge as anti-wisdom, and the pedantry of his two young tutors ('*Oiks*! Not *Bloody* Oiks!'), panicked that his bad memory will bring punishment down on them, emphasises its foolishness. Yet at the back of the fear, there's a valid resentment: we've already seen Jute's open, perhaps innocent face beguile a senior and arouse the chaplain. Brunning and Markland bully Jute because they know his looks will be coin and protection; that a pretty face, upraised, beseeching, has power in this place.

INTERIORS BY
JOCELYN HERBERT:
Sweat Room
counterculture

In a brown study

Travis's photo-wall

The Whips relax

FOUR TYPES OF GOTHIC:
Establishment

Theatrical

Disfigured

Madras

FILM STOCK SWITCH: WHY?
(From chapter one) for
emotional emphasis ...

... or economic convenience?

(From chapter three) for ethical contrast ...

... or to recall 'Free Cinema'?

(From chapter four)
to move from objective
study of ritual ...

... to subjective blaze
of romance?

(Also chapter four)
to ratchet levels of
fantasy up ...

... and up ...

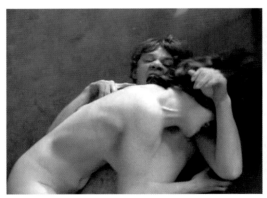

... and up ...

... or perhaps just to complicate them?

WATCHING/TARTING:
Denson

Wallace

Philips

The girl

Travis

Jute

Revolt's Posterboy
Today it's a set-design commonplace that the look of a room can be performative. In the late 60s, this trick was new to movies *and* student walls. A poster quickly tells the world who you – or the director – want people to think you are: Che, an elf, Hugh Hefner … Externalising himself, Travis cuts out a picture of a lion lazing in a tree; already the walls are thick with images of wars more familiar then perhaps than now.

If this generation felt penned in by ossified systems of knowledge, the bright new media consumables of the 40s and 50s seemed an easy path out, records most of all, representing spirit, challenge, vivid life, the recognition of conflict and the world.

Rock culture in particular stood for accessible sensual revolt against petrified tradition – but paradoxically, the record Travis plays and replays derives its presence from NOT being rock or pop. Howlett and Sherwin introduced Anderson to the 'Sanctus' from 'Missa Luba', released, and embraced by hipsters, in 1962: it's a Latin Mass sung by a Congolese boy choir, Les Troubadours du Roi Baudouin, under Father Guido Haazen. Why not rock or jazz? Prior to 1968, jukebox music was widely frowned on; even Free Cinema's fascination with jazz was coloured by left-ish suspicion of the products of American economic imperialism. Anderson didn't hate rock – Alan Price's life on the road would be inspiration *and* spine to *O Lucky Man!* – so did he simply intuit that an energy borrowed from the Stones (say) might bring with it unwanted associations, so that in after times the entire film would seem dated or parochial?

Travelling by touch, teaching himself to think and feel, Travis, a hipster himself, is ahead of the pop curve: made famous by *if…*. itself, the Sanctus can function as a blank slate, alien and open, gripping and mysterious. Not entirely blank: the dignity of the choir and the pressure towards unrealised agitation – just as Travis moves the needle back to the start, the 'jungle drums' begin – are qualities it cannot but inject into the film. But no Catholic God gets a look in: its words locked into Latin, this becomes a sound-only hymn to existential freedom and instinctive irresponsibility, sanctifying nothing but the hipster's dreams of resistance and escape. The original sleevenotes say it's sung in 'pure Congolese style' – 'pure' is nonsense, however. It's a syncretic collision of Europe and Africa, startling, evocative – and entirely shaped by colonial history. Baudouin was great-grandson of Leopold, the Belgian monarch responsible for the genocidal exploitation of the Congo in the 1900s – while the Congolese struggle for independence in the 1960s produced exactly the Sunday supplement war photography Travis has on his walls ...

Does Travis know all this? Does Anderson? However problematic it seems today, the assumption that 'African-ness' uncomplicatedly contested outmoded Eurocentric values was widespread in the 60s. And objects – above all bright pop-cultural consumables – which deliver such clear response in the moment often prove far more contradictory as time passes, as the instant assumptions they rest on lose coherence, as failures of purpose pile up. Symbols of ahead-of-the-curve become symbols of near-vacuous conformism: there are 'rebellious' poster-form readymades in every suburban bedroom anywhere. Ditto, in their time, the idealism and bold intention locked into and long lost in the flabby old bodies, the Victorian hymns, the Gothic windows, the Byzantine rituals of all-male discipline...

Latrine Grammar
'Biles, why are you such a freak?' Thus was the hapless Biles (Brian Pettifer) taunted by his fellows in the previous chapter. Now they chase him to ground in the gym and bear him away. As Wallace plays guitar in a doorless lavatory cubicle nearby, Biles's feet are tied to a cistern, his head down the bowl, and the bullies scamper off. Wallace sets him free, not very sympathetically. This location – actually at Aldenham School in Hertfordshire, where the shoot moved after Cheltenham – has a foul serendipity to it.

Choir, Confession, Control
In the ancient stones themselves tarry the ghosts of every discarded bad idea. Chantries were masses sung in choir schools funded, in perpetuity, by endowment. Until the Chantries Acts of the 1540s, the education of

the living (clever) poor depended on psalms sung for the souls of the wealthy dead. The Tudors dissolved this system to divert the cash – towards a Royal Navy, for example. A few 'grammar schools' were spared the full cull, the Tudor dynasty, by a typical irony, declared loving patrons of the transfigured remnants of the medieval institutions they had savaged. Thus the birth of the EPS, from class war and the first spasms of Empire.

'College is a symbol of many things,' the headmaster oozes – and it's true: buried under layers of pseudo-history, there's even the dream of the day a bourgeois Parliament cut off a monarch's head. But middle-class investment in the system also hides a more idealised act of dissent. The ambivalence we hear in sacred school song is the chantry's abiding phantom, the ghost of monkish resistance to a power grab long ago: it persists as a psalm sung within, for your *own* dead soul. Because insofar as the Arnoldian belief in the EPS as centre of moral and academic excellence marked a recognisable fact, it was ruthlessly instrumentalised – Empires need information clearing-houses, established centres of strategy, bureaus of knowledge-as-power. Thus the de-idealisation of the ideal: manhood will take Jute's voice from him, and his prettiness will fade, yet as moments of remembered possibility they will linger, piercing memories of the future you found yourself desiring when first you submitted to this strange sub-world: celestial song, not the 'adult' domain of Business Studies. Jute's pride in his young voice is his belief that he will grow up to bring beauty to this world from beyond it.

Yet the thread running through this whole chapter – the awkwardly dressed women ostracised in the chapel gallery, the head's 'sexy' joke, the cottaging hinted at in the latrine bullying scene – flips us in behind this 'beyond'. The reality of the power of the religious community is that it controls desire by projecting shame into it, which is to say the threat of being driven out, excluded, denied: like any utopia built on exclusion, the timeless sacred calm of universities and schools is a crust over a denial. The reality of the pretensions even of the ideal of all these inherited systems of wisdom is that – when they adapt to the realities of power in schoolroom and hallway, the realities of their survival in the world – they end with a chaplain physically abusing his charges and a child's head down a toilet.

Do Intertitles Alienate?

An actor in Brecht's Berliner Ensemble holds up a placard announcing the on-stage action – in *Mother Courage*, for example, declaring what will happen to the title character in the coming scene, along with relevant events from the Thirty Years' War – and the onlooker's perspective shifts: the audience is coaxed out of immersion into analysis, because to spot conventions, to recognise *why* a scene happens, is to begin to think. Thus the theory of *Verfremdungseffekt*, or 'alienation effect'. Anderson liked the technique, disliked this name for it: he felt alienation was a 'heavy word and not a very accurate one', since the point was not to put the audience off, 'but to *focus* their attention on what the scene is about'.[43] Probably a better word is 'defamiliarisation' – making fresh by making strange: if identification (via placards, asides, stylised gestures) does shift – from character *within* the plot to actor playing him – the viewer is nevertheless still beguiled, still engaged. The actor lets you know he knows what kind of character he's playing, what type of story, why things are how they are – *and so can you*.

A placard held up in a play is (or anyway was) a break with convention. In a film, it's an intertitle, routine silent-movie furniture. In a book, it's a chapter heading ('Term-Time' being *if*....'s third such). This film is also thick with jokes based on mannered physical gestures or attitudes, parodies of filmic body-cliché (*gests*, as they're called in Brechtian jargon): they're there to give the story revelatory spin, but until you're reminded to think of Brecht, they're so dry and private they may slip by unnoticed. Make things vanish by keeping them arty: did the fastidious Anderson invent the Invisible *Verfremdungseffekt*?

The Great Game

In Ken Loach's 1969 school-story film *Kes*, Brian Glover's teacher-referee, star striker among the tinies, thrusts himself brutally into their play: the rule-violation in his own favour a minor but nasty abuse of power. Mr Thomas, eager junior master in *if*... , is humbler. He too seizes the ball to run with it: tackled, he falls, wreathed in boys and smiles – and belongs. The camera is not cynical here: the new teacher's need to survive in this unfamiliar world is urgent. Unlike the football in *Kes*, the game in *if*.... is a bond: and of course it's rugby union, invented at Rugby School in 1823 by a local scholarship boy who 'with a fine disregard for the rules of football, as played in his time, first took the ball in his arms and ran with it, thus originating the distinctive feature of the Rugby game'.[44] The new rules spread fully across the imperial schooling system, the agreed variation marking the extent of a distinctive micro-society.

In *Tom Brown*, set in the 1830s, a different Rugby game is described: a free-for-all, with mismatched team sizes, players of all ages, and a site-specific, eccentric pitch. Such descriptions of unusual rituals – nostalgic, critical, exotic – were new to popular fiction in 1857: *Brown*, which is full of them, became a bestseller. Author Hughes, a radical MP battling against the incompetence of the rotten Tory squirearchy, immortalised Dr Arnold as a leader just and generous: 'What a sight it is, [exclaims a teacher] the Doctor as a ruler! Perhaps ours is the only corner of the British Empire which is thoroughly, wisely and strongly ruled just now.'[45] As Arnold battled to rid schools of horrid 'tradition' – bullying, flogging, fagging; terror, division – so the imperial order could be purged of venal stupidity. If Britain was to be a force for good in the world, its warriors must be saints; its schools must make them so.

Or else they can 'go fart in a bottle and paint it', as legendary *Brown* bully Flashman told Brown's bosom friend East during the Indian Mutiny, in George MacDonald Fraser's *Flashman in the Great Game*.[46] Thus do modern critics heap hilarious scorn on Arnold's moral vision. Anderson's attitude to all this is far less clear: is he against Empire altogether, or merely against its collapse into stupid market-compromised emptiness? Is Travis a Brown or a Flashman, a Stalky or a Che?

All the genre elements Hughes invented are here present (if no longer correct): dreams of a lost England; demand for enlightened,

civilised change; the urgency of moral quest (to risk, in this strange world, not becoming a man); the attachment of the masses – fags, 'scum' – to the customs which most oppress them; the pedagogic value of semi-lawlessness and self-rule; the fascination with the ethics of friendship – this last explored in *Brown* within a surprisingly shrewd, delicate and emotional context, of mutual homosocial fondness among boys, not to mention the practical value of hero worship. For Hughes the muscular Christian, this context was the

The very birthplace of manliness (*Tom Brown's School Days*)

very birthplace of manliness. *if....* – no less shrewd and delicate – is a good deal less wide-eyed.

A Fag's Life

The four Whips languidly drink tea and read while Philips toasts muffins for them, but their study is far from comfy. Its dreary walls square with *their* externalised identity: respectable historical paintings, sports teams, important buildings. As Philips leaves, the dynamic changes, Barnes and Fortinbras smacking lips at muffins and at Philips. Denson is outraged: 'This homosexual flirtatiousness, it's so *adolescent.*' Rowntree teases: 'What's the matter, Denson? Aren't you *keen?*' Then he barks into the corridor for the slave to be returned. If Rowntree is at ease with his own desire, Denson is prickly about his – but if this flirtatiousness *were* suppressed, then who knows what frustrations would build up. As a puritan, Denson is vulnerable – and must be punished, with exquisite Machiavellian subtlety, for not knowing (how) to play the game. Unless we're bigots too, we'll enjoy the humiliation that follows.

Fry Up†

There are memorable eating scenes in most Free Cinema documentaries, canteens signalling good companionship, bad nutrition, terrible taste. Here in a locker room in monochrome, a gaggle of boys supplement their atrocious official diet with a jolly Blytonesque panful of bacon and eggs, improvised low-culture democracy among the football boots. The Whips' formalised yet corrupt hierarchy seemed eavesdropped as accurately, but here the gaze – as it was in Free Cinema – is affectionate.

'Say Thank You'

When Philips returns, Rowntree again demonstrates the meaning of command, casually passing his young blond valet on to Denson. The screen enjoys this character – this actor, Robert Swann – and willingly grants him the charisma of his voice, his gestures, his bearing. To underestimate or deny the genuine ability to charm of the powers-that-be is to fail to grasp how they continue, in fact, to 'be' ...

Woman's Realm

In *Tom Brown* and *Stalky*, big issues are explored via the arguments of three close companions. Conversation here, lovingly unguarded, intimate, domestic even, is three non-connected monologues. Knightly (mum) reads from a woman's magazine, Wallace (daughter) worries about his looks, Travis (son) makes political declarations of an addlingly pretentious kind: 'War is the last possible creative act!' Their walls are a labyrinth of adolescent fantasy images.

'Resist any temptation to go into battle this month,' announces Travis's horoscope: 'Otherwise you risk not only being on the wrong side, but possibly in the wrong war.'

Denson the Whip enters without knocking, confiscates Travis's necklace of teeth, orders him to cut his hair – the command, as before, a meld of rage and repressed desire – and punishes them for drinking, which he didn't catch them doing. It's almost a defining trope of the school-story genre that unearned authority get its come-uppance. For Kipling in particular, serene non-conformist 'stalkiness' was a valuable byproduct of EPS stupidity: his trio are staunchly against official culture, utterly loyal towards – and amused by – one another. But it's the ridiculous protocols that make this fellowship possible, goading the best of youth into battle with them, to emerge strong and smart from the conflict.

The Wrong War
His face half-buried in his pillow, Denson peers animal-eyed at Philips. At Cheltenham in the 1930s the master-slave relationship of fagging routinely took sexual form, Anderson complacent on the arm of a handsome protective senior when Lambert first encountered him. By the 40s Anderson had resigned himself to his sexuality: he spoke little about it and liked it less, his adult life monastic in its austerity, if not celibacy. One of his signature themes as an auteur, Lambert suggests, was the unrequited crush on the safely married male lead: by which tactic, making *This Sporting Life*, he overrode (or overlooked) Richard Harris's rather obvious flaws as an actor. Utterly loyal as he is about his old friend's work, Lambert's attitude to this habit combines puzzled sorrow and a certain implied triumphalism; that by contrast he Lambert had lots of sex and boyfriends, and is still around and happy.[47]

Playwright Dan Rebellato has recently argued, cogently and forcefully, that the revolt following *Look Back in Anger* – which of course Anderson played a key role in – was partly grounded in a backlash against the pervasive gay subculture in British stage drama in the early 50s. George Devine at the RCT argued that 'the blight of buggery, which then dominated the theatre in all its frivolity, could be kept down decently by a direct appeal to seriousness and good intentions from his own crack corps of heterosexual writers, directors and actors.' In the film of *Anger*, the 'falseness of the [previous] theatrical era is explicitly linked with

An exterior masking a different interior: Noël Coward in *In Which We Serve* (Two Cities Films, 1942)

homosexuality, an exterior masking a different interior. Emotional dishonesty involves keeping your heart [in Osborne's words] "concealed, like Rattigan's and Coward's".' Rebellato cites Anderson's recollection of the Court style deriving from 'complete purity of feeling'. Of the Court, Anderson recalled, 'Its freedom from "camp" was total.'[48]

Rebellato shows that – at a time when homosexuality was almost never mentioned openly – Rattigan's and Coward's plays especially were rich in suave, coded exploration; but that as the queer threat evolved into a media obsession through the 1950s – a sinister, pervasive underworld was subverting the nation's manliness! – post-Osborne drama sought aggressively to heterosexualise itself. The Wolfenden Report of 1957 argued for liberalisation in private, a crackdown in public – its argument being that, stripped of the thrill of illegality, converted from a police to a medical matter, the problem would dwindle.[49] And a robustly unfrivolous theatre could provide a helping glare of limelight.

Of Albert Finney and Rachel Roberts in *Saturday Night and Sunday Morning*, Anderson was still saying, in 1986, that here was a 'sexuality, an unsentimental ruthlessness that jolted British cinema towards a new honesty'.[50] Thus the AYM-ist orthodoxy: sexual honesty is come. Think of it another way: the Kitchen Sink project as repressed middle-class theatricals cruising the lusty proles. 'All the gays at the Court,' said Anderson's RCT assistant,

> were closeted, and put up different smokescreens, Lindsay by attacking camp. I'm talking of a time long before the time of 'coming

Sexual honesty is come?
Richard Harris and Rachel
Roberts in *This Sporting
Life*

out' of course, but unlike the rest of us, Lindsay could only have come
out in theory. Once, when we were discussing his situation, Tony
[Richardson] said: 'I think we should push him into a Turkish bath and
leave him there.'[51]

if.... is not routinely placed in the canons of Queer Cinema.
Despite being suffused with male–male desire, it's not overtly camp and
it's certainly not militant – homosexuality isn't an 'issue', the characters
neither victims nor heroes in the sex wars. As resigned to misery as
Anderson clearly was, and as reticent about his own desire, he *had always
been* drawn to the survival strategies of those left behind, left out, left
stranded. Rebellato quotes Anderson disobligingly – that patrician tone
often so dislikeable – but in all this detailed and persuasive study, he
nowhere mentions Anderson's sexuality, and may oversimplify – even
misrepresent – Anderson's position. After all, celibacy was so far from
the acceptably dissident positions of sexual self-declaration in 1968, so
impossible to defend, that it may paradoxically have allowed Anderson a
clearer eye for the cruelties beneath the surface of so-called radicalism,
AYM-ist or Gay Lib. He despised the 'desperate middleclass craving to
cling to some – even fictitious – idea of hope, rather than be invigorated
by the truth',[52] but this scorn is here directed unexpectedly. Denson may
be unpleasant, but his crush – his hunger, his fear – is touched on in bitter
sympathy more than contempt. Recall the moment in one of Anderson's
beloved Free Cinema canteen scenes – in *Every Day Except Christmas*
back in 1957 – where the camera lingers on someone neither named or
explained. The voiceover:

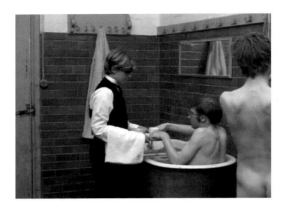

Tea boy and bathhouse:
Philips and Denson

Not everyone you find in Albert's works in the market – some you wonder where they come from. They come in at two or three in the morning, have a bite to eat, talk for a bit, and then they go. And you wonder where.

The someone in question, combing his hair to the gentle ribbing of others round him, is clearly effeminate, to be presumed gay. On the game and working another 'market'? Who knows? The atmosphere of this entire scene in *Christmas*, its 3am stillness, its yearning to belong, is overwhelming. Anderson's return to his own roots in *if....* is winningly gentle and unjudgmental in this regard at least; he's as Cowardist as Coward when he needs to be.

Pleasures, Punishments

Again the curious amalgam of sybaritic and squalid; the vulnerably intimate, the robustly communal. Denson takes his tea, served by his boy, in the bathhouse – civilised enough, except he's surrounded by naked showering bodies, some less buffed than others. Travis's prolonged cold shower is a deflected revenge for Denson's recent humiliation: this need to exercise authority is a sign of weakness, and a covert come-on. Anyway, being naked is only a trial if you're ashamed of your body, and Travis – beautiful in his anger – is not. This scene was one of very few censored in the UK and the US, where the new 'X' ratings system had arrived. Anglophones were denied their brief glimpse of youthful penis – Portugal and Greece, under the fascists, saw a great deal less.[53]

The Servility of Influence
From Ritual to Romance by Jessie L. Weston exists today as a brief
smothered squeak in the footnotes to Eliot's *The Waste Land*. Its almost
imperceptible presence here in this fourth chapter heading – 'Ritual and
Romance' – may just be a tiny mandarin joke, a phrase providing a jolt of
socio-cultural authority by its swanky provenance. It invokes Important
Art – not to mention the Quest for the Holy Grail – but surely it commits
us to nothing? In fact, this is a film full of similar subliminal hints and
indications.

Example: the hymn in the opening scene, 'Stand Up, Stand Up for
Jesus', invokes Anderson's great 1956 essay for *Sight and Sound*, 'Stand
Up, Stand Up', which Gavin Lambert called the 'critical equivalent of
Look Back in Anger', for attacking what Anderson called 'the kind of
philistinism which shrinks from art because art presents a challenge'.[54] In
'Notes for a Preface', the film's precursors are listed: Kleist, Brecht, Vigo,
Jennings and John Ford – 'old father, old artificer' he calls Ford,
Anderson here the former classics student blind-quoting Joyce blind-
quoting Ovid, another mandarin joke.[55] Connecting and connecting, he
wrote admiringly of Jennings: 'He had a mind that delighted in simile
and the unexpected relationship ... On a deeper level, he loved to link
one event with another, the past with the present, person to person.'[56]
And Anderson is quietly doing the same: underpinning – or undermining
– the didactic or philistine rush of the film's narrative energy, which
moves from stiflement to explosive release. By introducing such knots
and paradoxes, albeit at this near-subliminal level, Anderson seems to be
granting the viewer permission for much more ambivalent reflection.

There's a risk this avowedly anti-authoritarian film perhaps never
quite saves itself from: sometimes the robust mockery of and challenge to
one mode of authority silently swaps it for others. The bloodrush tug of
cinema, for example, privileges sexiness and energy, a hierarchy echoed
and affirmed by AYM-ism. While in a sub-world where careful, repeated
re-viewing is required, to uncover this dense weave of literary-scholarly
undercurrents, references and invocations, the Major Poet's voice now
and then shouts 'Scum' down the hallways of academe, and the Sweat
Room must present themselves as his jostling minions. A director making
a film about bad schooling and corrupt systems of authority – a film that
implicitly calls for a revolutionary transformation of the teacher–pupil
dynamic – can't simply wish away the issue of his own command over his
domain. To invoke Brecht as justification should be to take responsibility
for your own power over your own audience; even to transfer it. As

noted, the present-day cult consensus on *if....* is a little too smoothly self-pleased with itself entirely to confirm the success of this transfer.

Glass, Blankly†

Rowntree reads Deutoronomy: 'Surely this nation is a wise and understanding nation.' Once more the camera jumps from face to bored face, this time finding Travis. Maybe it takes a moment to pick him out: once you do, you find yourself assuming – from McDowell's unreadable intensity – that he's actually listening to this ritual for its content, for the power of the words, of Rowntree's voice. Then his gaze switches blankly away, to the marvellous biblical images in the windows: the switch from monochrome to colour becomes the switch from objective to subjective: we're inside Travis's head, and it's blazing and glorious and we have no idea what's going on.

A Horse Is a Horse†

And switch back to monochrome in the gym. What *does* the notorious change in film stocks mean? Look, it's simple, the money ran out – except ridiculous critics always need to 'interpret'. Well yes, *not quite*: time and budget running low, cameraman Miroslav Ondricek couldn't guarantee colour consistency filming in the chapel. Ondricek had been Anderson's cameraman on *The White Bus*, another 'poetic film, moving freely between naturalism and fantasy', its brief stabs of colour an aesthetic gamble its makers felt had worked. They decided to do it again here, and to make the changes where a change felt right. There *was* an artistic rationalisation: 'variation in the visual surface of the film would help create the necessary atmosphere of poetic licence', and 'in a film dedicated to "understanding", the jog to consciousness provided by such a colour change may well work a kind of healthy *Verfremdungseffekt*, an incitement to *thought*.' Lastly:

> Doesn't colour become more expressive, more remarked if drawn attention to in this way? The important thing to realise is that there is no symbolism involved in the choice of sequences filmed in black or white, nothing expressionist or schematic. Only such factors as intuition, pattern and convenience.[57]

Anderson had no time for auteur theory or semiotics, yet his film is a torrent of blink-and-miss contrary clues. Indeed, he insists on thought and understanding, pattern and intuition – yet in such a flood, the only route to a useable meaning must start with speculation. It's intriguing that the 'explaining-away' theory – 'All it means is the money ran out!' – has today taken such hold; it's not as if the reviews were falling over themselves to impose some strawman-foolish reading.[58]

Actually, as a narrative setup for what follows, the vaulting horse scene doesn't really gel into *any* convenient school of interpretation. Barnes, the recently ogling Whip, is benign here, unrecognisably teacherly. Even his exasperation at the weedier vaulters seems kindly. It's possibly the last scene which could plausibly have been in a Free Cinema documentary, back when innocence was an option – and by deliberately tamping the sex intensity of this moment back to 50s levels, the desire suffusing the scene which follows is heightened.

Watching†

The context of expressed tenderness in *Tom Brown* is something Fraser's *Flashman* books robustly distance themselves from: not 'manly' enough perhaps, at least in that wised-up, post-Wolfenden, post-Bond sense, when the ever-present homosocial reality in the Canonic Public School Story suddenly became a 'problem', to be disavowed or sniggered at. One of the deep strengths of *if....* is the assured richness of its grasp of the male-on-male *continuum* of such a world, from actively gay (present-day sense) to every kind of other, more ambiguous, less committed queer space, as convenience, as 'ideal family', as experiment among siblings, as serene comforting companionship.

Philips puts on his sweater, tidies his tousled fringe, watches Wallace from the balcony, ever aware he radiates allure. Wallace gives Philips a het-coquette over-shoulder glance and grin, then leaps into his beautiful slow-motion gymnastic dance in the air – and the music shifts, from soft pulse-blood drumming to poised chords defying gravity. This is an excellent instance of the Andersonian (rather than Brechtian) body-cliché gag. In a mainstream love story, all this would seem business-as-usual, dreamy girl falling for athletic boy. But here, Wallace is the flirt, performing so as to be cruised. The younger boy – gazing, still – does the choosing, the older – active member in a revolutionary trio – does the hoping.

Real Blood†

Perhaps any scene in any film can be described as ritual, or romance, or both. In 1968, this question was Nouvelle Vague territory – what to do with the screen conventions of flirt and fight? Truffaut's *Jules et Jim* (1961) also contains a fencing scene, with wall-bars and the oath of loyalty seeding the *ménage à trois* which, despite being unstable and doomed, we desperately want to believe in, see survive.

Is this simply coincidence? The acoustics muffle all reference harvesting, till the scene – especially in sudden colour in the battered squash court – points only at itself. You struggle to catch what's being yelled, swashbuckling clichés from the Romantic lexicon as foils flash – 'Death to tyrants!' 'What dies if England live?' – or from Byron's *Childe Harold*, as Travis swings in like Fairbanks on a gym-rope: 'War! Even to the knife!' 'Essentially,' insists Anderson, 'the heroes of *if....* are, without knowing, old-fashioned boys ... traditionalists. It is they, not their conformist elders nor their conformist contemporaries, who speak the tongue that Shakespeare spoke.'[59] Or is this Anderson's critique of self-adoring schoolboy pretentiousness – a new slant on blocked, inarticulate Kitchen-Sink fury, the words mouthed, but not understood? Compare the headmaster's degraded jargon, the meanness at the heart of Rowntree's stylishly delivered speeches. Of course if it's an attack, it's also fun to watch, a loving image of energy and friendship and Zenda-like play-acting, except with voices masked by bad acoustics. It ends not in tears, but – suddenly, physically – with the thrill of a slashed and bloody hand: '*Real blood!*'

Sauce

From piratical play whirlwind to romancing Mrs Kemp at table's end. Wallace and Knightly offer her water, salt, spinach – then Travis leans close, tray in hand, leer on face: 'Dead Man's Leg, Mrs Kemp?' Sexual slang? Inspired shock-surrealist invention? She remains vague, vacant, quarantined in her zonked disconnection – the phrase is actually routine post-war school slang for unidentifiable meat, but it's almost stronger if you *don't* know this. Smirking, Travis jerks a phallic bottle of Daddy's Sauce at her: 'Do you need this, Mrs Kemp?' The bell, and Rowntree interrupts the non-exchange: 'Cheering at college matches has degenerated completely!' All must attend, so instead Travis and Knightly bunk off into normal film narrative at last – or fantasy, if that's what it is.

No Great Escape

While Wallace attends the match, cheering alongside a frenzied matron, the other two, running far out of bounds, disturb traffic, upset workmen and passersby, and steal a motorbike. Two spoiled teens wrecking a sales clerk's day – but framed so that we cheer, one in the eye for the system! The geography of the canonic school story extends beyond the school: Tom Brown and Stalky spend much time lolling in masterless bucolic bliss. Fundamental to the psychic geometry of these stories is the treatment of outsiders, as valets, serfs and patsies. To face down myriad insurgents, the Empire breed (Kipling's term), bonding over shared time of tribulation – bad food, worse sex, unmentionable loneliness – learned to bear themselves as lordlings. Hence the uneasiness of the genre's survival into the present: post-68, even outsiders *within* England were really no more inclined to be deferential than insurgents overseas.

Isn't this why, as an attempted metaphor for Vietnam – never so claimed by Anderson, often proposed by others – *if....* is a failure? Flashman in the *Flashman* novels – similarly sardonic, Jagger-style, end-of-the-60s, antihero material – confronts school-story romanticism with unvarnished imperial catastrophes. We're straight away taken outside 'our' (Tom Brown's) moral world, and right *into* 'Vietnam' (actually 1840s Afghanistan). Whatever the Vietcong were in 1968, they were *not* the sentimentalised romantic hero-rebels of a canonic school story: Fraser's 'natives' are flawed and wily and agenda-led, no patronising fantasy projection of saintliness, his mockery of today's *and* yesterday's political correctness – Flashman's racist, sexist, an anti-reform Tory, an outrageously self-centred liar, coward and fraud – paradoxical in its pragmatic respectfulness (since everyone's as bad as everyone else). Our rebels break out of school, but not out of the metaphor: do they ever even engage with the imperialist 'other', the embattled native masses excluded from *any* rule over their own lives?

Rural Rides

Hippolyte Taine was greatly impressed with the freedom EPS boys had to wander the surrounding countryside in the 1860s, contrasting it with the French situation. By comparison with the children in *Zéro*, hemmed in as much by the ugly town as the school, the boys in *if....* (even with Jocelyn Herbert painting their walls) scarcely know their luck. Nevertheless, their solitary day of pastoral idyll is a ritual trope snipped out of Kitchen Sink and pasted into the school story. Camera tight on the speeding duo, we travel at their pace, the pace of freedom, on open roads past rolling gold-green fields, through still-living avenues of elms and the lost English summer. Wilkinson's music, with its jazz orchestral texture, is probably the only element here that wasn't on the way to becoming a cliché.

Girl-as-Gag†

As they enter the deserted 'Packhorse Café', lush colour switches to monochrome. There are similar schoolboys-in-friendly-pieshop scenes in *Brown* and *Stalky*, except here the lusty peasant lass is bored, sullen, at *best* indifferent towards her customers, who slouch – each with subtly different body language – at the counter. Not bothering to charm, Travis checks out her rear then snatches a kiss. She squirms away and slaps him hard – a replay of the hefty, heartfelt blow which at audition won Christine Noonan *and* McDowell their roles, according to Sherwin.[60] Into this instant explodes almost all we'll ever learn of her passions, her boredoms, her beliefs, aims, needs. As the scene continues, she's drawn into the myth-ridden perspective of their quest, her presence – solitary representative of the oiks and the town tarts, of wretched life out beyond the logic of this enclosed sub-world – almost immediately ambiguous, more symbol than agent. Three body gags help this process: outside, Travis pats his bike like a cowboy his mount; inside, while making coffee, the girl glances over her shoulder at the boys, through a thick, ink-black curtain of hair – then slides the coffees down the counter, the saloon girl in a Western. A familiar sign of sexual come-on – we just saw Wallace use it – bumps into the ritual shtick of a different kind of romance entirely.

Threesomes†

The power of the scene is *not* the sudden nudity, *not* the banter (about tigers), *not* the music ('Missa Luba' on the jukebox). Nakedness had the free pass of anti-censorship novelty in 1968, but animal growling followed by sexplay to hot drum-pop has today long been deeply un-special industry ritual. Ten thousand successors make the grappling seem clumsy, even though McDowell and Noonan play it likeably enough – a document of two pretty young things actively enjoying the moment,

Hidden intensity of feelings: Knightly

enjoying their own daring – but what makes it stay in the mind is the well-named Knightly's quiet third-wheel presence. His is the heartbreakingly exact moment: blond, shy, sad, the intensity of his feelings towards Mick well hidden, he sits, *not* watching (compare Denson's gimlet-eye on Philips), and carefully places Travis's saucer over the cup to keep his hero's coffee warm. When the couple come to the table, the girl ruffles Knightly's hair and, looking at Travis, says: 'I like Johnny.' This sequence is highly charged and in some ways very strange.

The trace memory may again be the *ménage* in *Jules et Jim*, that groundbreaking portrayal of women and love – but if conscious, the reference to Truffaut's dialectic of kindness and hardness, devotion and betrayal, is at maximum compression. Jeanne Moreau plays a 'complicated' proto-feminist who wants to live out 'male' (stereotypically active) and 'female' (stereotypically passive) prerogatives simultaneously, captivating and draining her companions. We're on the edge of the sexual revolution – yet Anderson's girl is a cipher, because only this way can Anderson consider her Travis's *equal*. 'The essence,' according to Sherwin, 'of a certain kind of casual meeting' – the anonymous bar pick-up and backroom fuck.[61]

Noonan would appear briefly in *O Lucky Man!* – but then left the industry, never to be tracked down by fanzines or researchers. Word of mouth has it she loathed making *if....*, her pubic exposure presumably helping to get the film its 'X' rating. Her character has no name: borderline chauvinism or Brechtian device? Travelling on intuition himself, Anderson didn't always explain himself much to his players – and besides, McDowell apparently first suggested the nakedness. So did Noonan afterwards come to feel exploited or humiliated? Press reports of the time have her unbothered, amused at the fuss, including her husband's grumble: 'Oh God, you're not going to be one of those titty actresses.'[62]

To show us a girl and a boy matched in freedom, her mirror his mirror, self-obsessed animals of perfectly reflected vanity, Anderson chooses to invoke full adolescent cruisiness, the brotherly love-in of the all-male utopia, where anyone does anyone and no hearts get hurt. Stonewall is no more 'outside' culture than Salford or the Noble Savage of middle-class thrill-seeking – but this ubiquitous 60s delusion has wrapped the scene in misreading. The orthodoxy was that real sex was always liberation – as if the zipless junglefuck releases us from history, which is to say, compromise – but monkish Anderson, if he often went along with this orthodoxy, stayed ever suspicious about what arrives when repression 'ends', keeping even this moment of apparent emotional utopia in quotes.

'Ritual and Romance' is the film's first problem chapter: the interplay of gesture, convention and parody – from Westerns, from swashbucklers, from wherever – is so intricately connected that it falters into overload and clots. Anderson is *so* unwilling to be seen as sentimental that he only presents such material in ways he can disavow, as quasi-spoof. It's not that his imagined freedoms are clichés, rather that he thinks freedom must include freedom from cliché, and has to pallisade the moments where it's achieved with the clichés it escapes. If freedom imagined simply means a musical interlude bike riding in a field, well, *Butch Cassidy and the Sundance Kid* (1969) is just round the corner: certainly Anderson is too sceptical – allergic to ritual, terrified of the risks of a genuine shared language – not to insert flashes of dissent into his fantasy, but as they get more subliminal they become less coherent. The new sexual 'openness' has thoughtful life only if it protects itself with ever more private versions of Coward's coded camp nuance, apparently, but Anderson had long seceded from belief in the latter.

Homework
From this travelling swirl of fantasy codes back to tight documentary style, a high shot through a window back down into the contained world of school. This entire chapter – the fifth, 'Discipline' – takes place within stone walls.

On Patrol†
To fit *within* the school's ambit of fake tradition, a car must be immobilised. Mr Thomas is busy beneath his when Denson challenges him: eager for approval, the newcomer is apologetic. The Whip – the warder – is polite but cold: 'You won't be long, will you, sir?' It's more an order than a question: the strange sub-world is to be maintained, not the means to escape it. (And assuming the film stock switch wasn't just a matter of convenience, the black-and-white here buttresses unreality-as-prison, not imagination-as-flight.)

Post-coital Drag†
A scene to deepen confrontations – because in canonic terms, smoking is always an 'issue'. Indeed, in *Eric, or Little by Little*, it's the inevitable drug-precursor to stealing and death, via 'beastliness', that fine Victorian code for gay sex (poking fun at this specific logic, *Stalky* cheerfully approved the illicit cheroot). Cigarettes in a twilit setting – but the

Equality of
companionship:
Wallace and Philips

innuendo is *very* light, more than dispelled by Denson's jealousy and spite. Wallace and Philips may be lovers, but it's Denson's total lack of ease at an unbullying desire that's perverse, his fear of any relationship that's free – in all its amiable banality – from the system's values or control. With racks of guns as backdrop, this need for snatched privacy, this equality of companionship – the younger boy admonishing the older for his lack of ambition – has intimacy and grace. What's so threatening is that it's so *un*threatening, so wholly unremarkable. In an early draft, the uprising was a response to Wallace's expulsion for this dalliance (earlier still, the dalliance was Travis's). Gorgeous in body, Wallace is otherwise bland, the most passively amiable of the rebels – also he's distinctly non-'gay' in stereotypical cinematic coding, then or since.[63]

Laughter, Cancer, Truth
No scene occurs as often in *Stalky* as its rebel trio giggling themselves limp, at schemes gone awry, at their own foolishness, at the world's. Laughing beyond all control is hard to act, and not *that* convincingly executed here – though the sense of its being forced probably helps the atmosphere of stifled boredom. The hilarity arises from a teen discussion of the worst possible kind of death. 'Being flayed alive!' suggests Travis, gleefully: 'That's what the Crusaders did to their enemies. They used to send their neatly folded skins back to their victims' wives.' Then there's Knightly's mother, whose cancer took six months. In contrast to the bogus holiday tales he and Travis swapped half the film ago, this sudden mumbled detail is piercing and unexpected in its truthfulness.

Indomitable

Over fruit and cheese, the Whips drink port with Mr Kemp, and discuss the House. Rowntree laments its dullness, warns of a 'certain hardcore in the studies', and proposes action. 'The headmaster doesn't like too much thrashing,' says Kemp the powerless figurehead, but Rowntree insists.

Lambert condemns the Whips – premature yuppies, proto-Thatcherites – as 'betrayers of their own generation'; yet to Anderson they're 'conformist'.[64] The difference is telling: Anderson was far less enthusiastic than his old friend about the changes the 60s wrought. Lambert's appeal to a *generational* morality misses an obvious point – as villains, the Whips are handsome; Rowntree has élan and confidence: yuppies as radical Thatcherite institution-smashers were *products* of the 60s, not foes.

Among many things at work in *if....* is a clash of styles and generations – of worldviews, assumptions, practices – as embedded in technique itself. Common to Lowe's and Anderson's life stories is the rise of a common anger at the loss of a cultural heritage: both despaired of the shallow, careless present. 'If Arthur had a good part,' Anderson said years later, 'nobody would be better. He was really one of our finest actors.'[65]

Lowe was eight years Anderson's senior, an old-school Tory to the latter's quasi-leftist – but they admired one another, and were not altogether dissimilar: the anarchic streak, the guardedness, the dry humour. Both were from a time being foreclosed by history. Lowe's subsequent emergence in *Dad's Army* – as focus of the greatest ensemble television-comedy team of the age – reflects what Anderson valued in him: his professional skill at the projection of an unmistakable 'type', combining absurdity, pathos and – paradoxically – the indomitable. In *This Sporting Life*, he shines; while he was alive, Anderson never made a film Lowe wasn't in. The roles are small, but central.

Certainly Lowe had little sympathy with the adolescent rebellion *if....* approves – his tremendous professionalism, his self-abnegating

Anderson and Lowe on set for *The White Bus*; Lowe's Mr Kemp as consummate clown

commitment to the material and techniques of his craft, are the matter of *his* resistance. Against the pitiless shove of youth consumer-culture — emphasis on firm, sexy bodies, the zest of the unfettered instantaneous — Lowe tops this scene, and hollows it out, with a consummate clown's moment. If Kemp is delinquent about his human responsibilities, the Whips crowding him into rubber-stamping measures he dislikes, his inner world now suddenly dwarfs everything visible: Lowe takes a mandarin pig and pops it into his mouth. Perfect comedy business from an actor hired to play a 'Lowe-type' character: maybe the Whips master the narrative, even the *mise en scène*, but Lowe just looked out into your heart.

Out-Flanking

'The thing I hate about you, Rowntree, is the way you give Coca-Cola to your scum and your best teddybear to Oxfam, and expect us to lick your frigid fingers for the rest of your frigid life.' By schoolboy standards, this language is polite. Odd and memorable as this sentence is — not to say fetishistic and ridiculous — it presumably evolved as censor-dodging euphemism. 1968 saw censorship transformed: no more Lord Chamberlain's approval for plays; the 'X'-rating system for films. Fingers are hardly the proverbial body-spot we lick, perhaps, but actually the substitution works better than any uncensored Osbornian bluntness. His position requires Rowntree know how desire shapes the surface and the depths, yet Travis directly challenges him here, at once seeing all and belittling all. The three are called to execution, down the empty, echoing corridors of a prison flick.

Licked?

The punishment ritual takes place in the room of first blood and true love: the gym. Beaten, Wallace shambles back for Travis to check the damage: blood again, rueful grin. The non-British world persists in being shocked *and* amused at the tenacity of flogging in the nation's psyche — as Hippolyte Taine noted, when the authorities at Charterhouse in the 1840s had threatened to end birching and institute fines, the boys went on strike.

The sensibility will pervade British pop culture till the late 70s at least, most outlandishly in Jimmy Edwards's mainstream TV comedy-slapstick series *Whacko!* (1956–60), where a mortarboarded headmaster's single pleasure is the mass caning of his boys — a 1960 spin-off movie was called *Bottoms Up*, the entire phenomenon so flagrant it makes you wonder how anyone was *ever* taken in by closeting.[66]

Topping Fun

'Everybody knows,' says the enabler of the scene that forms the greater part of Pat Califia's notorious long short S&M story 'The Calyx of Isis', that 'it's really the bottom who runs the scene' – the 'bottom' there being the kidnapped slave, who proves her loving trust in her owner (or 'top'), by submitting willingly to some sixty pages of binding, whipping, fisting and more at the hands of a supergroup of seven iconic types of lesbian dominatrix, only one of whom she's ever met.[67]

At the heart of Califia's politics of S&M is an absolute: that everyone involved be clear-eyed and consensual, that the utopian loving fit of difference (of desire, of capacity) emerges from a basis of equality, a radically democratic root. As a description of the real world, this is an idealised dream, naturally – the perfect functioning of the idea of informed consent the political quest. 'Some people cannot be trusted with a helpless body. You know who you are,' writes Califia in the introduction to *Macho Sluts*, the 1988 collection that first made 'Calyx' widely known. 'Some people don't choose to take responsibility for the pain they inflict on others. Some people think it's kinder to ignore a need they don't understand, to starve someone in the name of decency or equality or love.'[68] As an ideal against which to study Travis's beating and symbolic gang-rape – and to tease out the delusions of the various characters and possibly the director – Califia's model is as invaluable as it's paradoxical.

A climax has been reached in a contest of styles of *command*. The three are beaten: after four strokes, the number his fellow rebels received, Travis straightens, grabs his jacket – but the ordeal is not over. Voice high and tense, Rowntree orders he wait until told, and 'get down': he is the

The tenacity of flogging in the nation's psyche (*Bottoms Up*, Transocean Films, 1960)

focus of passionate extra attention – ten strokes in all – while the sound of every further run-up and brutal connection peals out, in agonising real time, across the studies and the Sweat Room. As he's slammed repeatedly against the equipment by the force of the blow, we see Travis's sang-froid crumble. On departure, he must, says protocol, shake Rowntree's hand and thank him: humiliation is complete.

Or is this highly ritualised S&M etiquette? What if the bottom *is* running this scene? After all, Travis is enduring a pain he called on himself. And it's Rowntree that cracks: flushed and heavybreathing, he's suddenly slave to his own loss of self-command. Far beyond straightforward provocation and punishment, haven't we in reality been watching a complex flirtation, a Jagger-camp Travis daring Rowntree to step outside the safety zone of his official role into a relationship between equals – and not the soft-focus vanilla of the gunroom tryst either, or even the tigergrowl cruise-and-grappling of the café?

Travis's most provocative facial expression is McDowell's most used: a mask of wide-eyed innocence – his deft and sexy and cheeky elegance as he opens the gym doors with a flourish, removes his jacket in the fluid, elegant move we saw before, throws his dandyism in hierarchy's face. Giving Rowntree even the grown-up ghost of a

The politics of S&M: from insolent flirtation to defeat, or from humiliation to conquest?

manipulative Jute-eye come-on is pure prick-tease – and the scene ends with Travis bent over the bar, tears in his eyes, Rowntree crashing into him from behind.

At issue, consent. In S&M theory, violence – as a consensual game – *is the bond*: thus a perfectly achieved equality of relationship, whatever the activity, whatever the system. In a game, the 'slave' can run the scene. In reality, in the world that isn't a game, are terrorists actually ever genuinely at war with systems of power? Don't they rather *depend* on them, passive-aggressively affirm them, unconsciously conspiring to sustain the rule of the rulers – flawed, human, out of control – with their non-defeat defeats? 'These normal things, normal to every high school to some degree or another,' wrote Frank Kogan about Columbine, of terror, of bullying, of stratification: they're what society wants school to be for, to reproduce itself. To overestimate the self-knowledge of the powers-that-be is to declare your secret allegiance, complicity, capitulation: 'It hurt less to kill people and finally to kill themselves.'

Elsewhere, meanwhile, Peanuts looks into his microscope and watches bacilli multiply. The child thrown onto his own resources in the EPS – from Tom Brown to Jute – *is not consenting*.

🖲 🖲 🖲

It Killed the Ancient Romans

A stumbling translation, a bad guess, a reliable pupil told to 'look it up': the classical 'construe' is a comedy staple of the canonic school story – and the 'relevance' debate was whiskered 150 years before the late 60s assault on educational fossilisation. In the 1830s, Dr Arnold wanted to vary Rugby's traditional lesson-diet with subjects like mathematics. In the 1860s, the Clarendon Commission failed to persuade Parliament to modernise the Nine – old boys in Commons and Lords invoked 'tradition' to head off the threat. In the 1890s, *Stalky* made a running gag of the banter between classics and science teachers. Here in the sixth chapter, 'Resistance', the teacher – Charles Lloyd Pack, squat and snowy-haired – barely engages with his charges: to protect his love of his subject, he's dug a psychological trench of near-rote response and incongruous dark glasses.

Meanwhile Anderson replays *his* favourite gag: the invisible *Verfremdungseffekt*, in which a speech – amusing colour in its immediate context – comments on the story as a whole. The history teacher, Rowntree reading in chapel, Knightly's horoscope for Travis – and here the passage being translated from Plato's *Republic*, which advises a community give its whelps a blooded view of war. But no one twigs. The Sixth learn Greek because Greek is what you're taught in the Sixth, the links between knowledge, wisdom and understanding long broken, even the once-sensible imperial pretext – yesterday's Empire-builders carefully studying their classical predecessors – now a ghost of itself. The imitation has passed from decline beyond fall.

Democracy Wall

Anderson, said production designer Jocelyn Herbert, was 'suspicious of design', and her *if....* interiors are an absurdist symphony in drab; as severe as her RCT stage sets, in fact. Design was but an adjunct to the author's intentions, as policed by director: text was God, the director its vicar on earth, and Herbert – such was her self-denying ordinance – was nicknamed the 'invisible designer'.[69]

But if the school's austerity reflects its inhumanity, what does Anderson's austerity reflect? What visual pleasures does he ever allow *his* charges, the audience? There's only richness when the backdrop's clutter interrupts the foreground's iron control: the dialectic of obedience and freedom sedimented into Gothic architecture, for example, or the prefabricated images – of mainstream celebrity and consumption – on study or Sweat Room walls, where allegiance and possibility can be expressed: here we learn things about the people we're watching, including all manner of contradictions or collusions they may not themselves see. At the RCT, the text-God was the script – but there's just as much story locked up in these pin-ups and pointy arches, not to mention the counter-narratives in the music, to triangulate with the dreams or faiths or passions or politics of a community wider than what's in the heads of any characters encountered at the written or acted levels. Repeated re-reading will amplify the clash in such secondary layers of meaning; just as it tends to nudge more conventional sections of plot back below the horizon of conscious study.

With bored concentration, Travis fires his darts at his pin-ups. Meanwhile – behind him, and not a target – a famous photo of Lenin disguised as a grinning worker, with wig and floppy cap. Cinema's intrinsic politics are unavoidably more present-day democratic than that of most art forms – only modern pop outflanks it – because it contains so many different, unintegrated 'coding systems', conflicts and betrayals the director may not be consciously aware of, and can never stop from colliding, as equals, in (or with) the viewers' minds. There's far more here than just Anderson's angry revenge on his own school roots: he's taking reflective and/or intuitive potshots at his entire self-directed education, via his self-selected mentors and collaborators. We are not out of Free Cinema, still less Kitchen Sink – cloisters for back-to-backs, fantasy for documentary, the dandified unspoken for Richard Harris's inarticulate emotional yells – and yet *if*.... also takes frustrated aim at all of them. Does Anderson *really* think Travis is the Lenin in this story? Or is this another symbol of the futility of the public schoolboy's pretensions, the speed-read-if-you-spot-how equivalent of a Che poster?

'House Thump'

Boys pound fists on tables, to mark a meaningless triumph. We should not kid ourselves that the rebels are rebelling against anything of cultural value, rather a brutish tribal silliness.

Bullets, Oath, Mutiny

This time the trio blood themselves deliberately – each cuts his thumb with a razor. The act of cutting may be faked; the viewers' twinge of empathy isn't, as Anderson's gift for intense real-time physicality reaches a climax. The whelps are brought to war, though, as in *The White Bus*, the casualties that follow might as well be dummies. 'The whole world will end very soon,' declared Travis, many scenes ago, with blankly melodramatic relish. The Great Rugby Mutiny took place in 1798, the year Butler took charge at Shrewsbury. A schoolboy shooting corks at windows, a flogging, a revenge, a mass fine, an uprising with real guns. The headmaster – Henry Ingles, known to legend as the 'Black Tiger' – had his study door blown off its hinges, his books and furniture torched; the boys were besieged on an island by local militia, armed, while a JP read the Riot Act. Order restored; ringleaders expelled.

Beds/Twin

In a tiny bedroom, Mr Kemp sits pyjama'd at bed's edge and sings a madrigal, to his wife's recorder: 'Cupid from his favourite nation/Care and envy will remove.' The specifics of the sex lives of others are often amusing, but if this scene played *merely* to 60s pop-cult orthodoxy – the teen-fascist cliché that, no longer a secret adults-only activity, sex now belonged to the young alone – it would be bullyingly cruel: emasculated, ageing loser; frigid, childless ice maiden. Instead it's a private island of curiously ambivalent tenderness, surrounded by youthful ugliness of spirit. Anderson understood – and scrupulously refused to despise – isolation, incompatibility, beached modes of resistance.

Beds/Single

According to editor David Gladwell, one of the few scenes filmed but not used was a dream sequence with boys running in slow motion into matronly arms.[70] Matron, this likeably dotty St Trinians figure, briskly diminutive, ludicrous, smiles as she dozes in an armchair, hand at breast, and you can read what you will – of sexual or romantic or innocent dreaming – into her inner life. Disastrous conflict is – by the system's own design – inevitable, declares the film as a whole. The counter-insistence in this sequence of fleeting but unforgettable scenes is generous and lovely, that other, perhaps unknowable, dreams and spaces of resistance *will* persist, that we all of us also wall off part of our being from *either* side. These are the scenes that stay in the mind, their secret force gathering with every replay.

Beds/Shared†

If the girl functions somewhat as an honorary gay man in *if....*, Philips's and Wallace's love story is far more stylised as being, well, straight. The pair lie unsexually peaceful under a single blanket in a dormitory full of sleeping boys, a scene with a sweetness and unphysical innocence that – more even than the motorbike-music-*ménage* interlude – hails from way

Modes of resistance: solo, paired, silly and sublime

over on the idealised side of mainstream romantic cinema coupledom, Anderson here the admiring pupil of John Ford's *My Darling Clementine* (1946).

Of Stars in Sullen Mass†

Philip Bagenal's Peanuts, the beanpole boffin with rat-filed teeth, is an intriguing character, aloof yet somehow attractive. He ends the first chapter with a cool warning – 'Paradise is for the blessed, not the sex-obsessed' – and seems actually to be the only person in the movie in undisenchanted pursuit of knowledge, a scientist (seemingly self-taught) and a Buddhist (clearly self-taught). Acknowledging a fellow refusenik, Travis shows Peanuts the bullet and offers to initiate him in the revolt – but astrophysics dwarfs such petty human projects: 'Space, you see, Michael, is all expanding at the speed of light. It's a mathematical certainty that somewhere out there – among all those millions of stars – there's another planet where they speak English.' But Travis turns the telescope away from abstract cosmic speculation to a nearby – imaginary? – window, where the girl brushes her hair, then waves to him. As with the history teacher's scene, the resistance to exchange is mutual, a refusal of equals, two technologies of violence passing as ships in the night. The poetic compression of the idea is brilliantly judged, and – because they agree to differ yet maintain respect – it's a likeable scene. In its quiet way, it's also pivotal – at its heart is Anderson's usual bleakness about incompatibility, and the inevitable non-arrival of wisdom and understanding. Bagenal auditioned after seeing the ad in *Melody Maker*, which asked for boys who wanted to be stars – thousands answered the ad, but his (says Sherwin) was the only speaking part cast this way.[71] From a Brechtian perspective, Peanuts – the knowing observer at the centre of the story – is the film's secret non-tragic hero.[72]

On Being Recruited†

'You're all *meat* – ' shouts the chaplain, dressed as a soldier, ' – to be punished!' But of course it's 'meet' adj not 'meat' noun: as far as the chaplain knows, the explosions to come will all be fake. He no more comprehends actual blood than he comprehends actual harm. Besides, he has other things on his mind, leans forward in creepy intimacy and directs his sermon – on desertion – at Jute alone. And Jute swings round in his seat to return the gaze. Another over-the-shoulder come-on? If so, it's by far the most disturbing – Jute is clearly still a child. Gavin Lambert, writing of boarding schools in the 1930s, makes sharp distinction between the gay adults who helped boys discover their true sexuality – Lambert himself barely a teenager when his music teacher seduced him[73] – and predator-perverts with a different agenda. The question of the consensual again – and of the hidden complicity between rebels and authority. This is the film's most open, present-tense moment of life-changing *decision* – bright and centre-screen against the darker floor and backs of heads here, no other so vivid or visible, is Jute's pale, freckled, worried little face that of a victim, or is his childish manipulation, for the sake of belonging, being manipulated in its turn, exploited and corrupted by the brotherhood he's choosing to be induced into? Of course it's far too oblique to be interpreted definitively: this is why it's so unsettling.

Other Rooms†
While the boys are off playing at war, Mrs Kemp wanders their dormitories naked, childless and desolate. She's curvy, wide-hipped, far from the toned hard-body conventions of present-day glamour, and her vulnerability makes the image all the more powerful. The censorship battles of the late 60s were already as much sales device as expressive necessity, but this scene is something quite different, a small madness and a large sadness as a further mode of resistance, a retreat into the painterly and the gestural, as if she was some mythical goddess of sterility. Anderson thought Sherwin's original idea – to score this scene with a marching army's feet – was too heavy-handed:[74] this counterpoint, by edit rather than sound overlay, is more elliptical, unsettling again: the insanities presented – Mrs Kemp versus war – seem to be opposites, but they merge into the same unstoppable thing.

Two sides of the insanity of war: motherless child ...

Wargame
The soldiers are kids clambering over the roofs of corrugated iron shacks. The explosions are paltry, the woods a tidy, timid no-man's-land. It hadn't yet broadcast in spring 1968, but today you think *Dad's Army*, and laugh. At one point, the trio are ambushed by Mr Thomas, still desperate to be liked, to belong. The grown-up tosses a tiny bomb at them and the boys pretend-die in slow motion, their sarcasm lost over his head. A little before, they came on Peanuts the savant, critical of his troop's unscientific bayonet-charging, lecturing on the Brechtian *gest*: 'It's awful, you forget to yell. The Yell of Hate. It's the yell that counts.' Or maybe his telescope really was a ray gun all along.

Returning Fire
The trio shoot up the tea urn, but the oppressed don't rise, not the bullied juniors, not even Mr Thomas. The chaplain shows tremendous courage striding out to confront this menace. Perhaps it's just failure of imagination. Travis shoots him anyway, and prepares to bayonet him. As we watch the victim squirm and plead, do we glimpse Anderson's own fate, 45 himself in 1968, at the thoughtless young hands of those *he's* shaped, created, bullied even? Free Cinema and Kitchen Sink and AYM-ism combined to call up The Beatles and the student generation – working-class youth, once sullen objects of the audience gaze, now making and nearly controlling their own culture, their own versions of their own aspirations and self-image ... The whole ungrateful mass youth convulsion sweeping everything away that Anderson made, pushing him into middle age, out of sympathy, out of fashion, directing sequels that weren't even proper sequels.[75]

... and prophet armed

The chaplain's wriggling lasts a very long time – first it becomes 'acting', then it becomes difficult to watch. Which means we start to think of him as human, in our space, and not just a character. We *are* all meat: and thus heir to pain and fright and – right here, right now – utter loneliness in the face of one's own death. But myths are hard to unmake, as Peckinpah discovered with his balletic slow-motion cowboy deaths. Yes, some of us pity, and some of us snicker – and the device to make the scene feel *real* turns back into special effect. Schools have always been the neighbourhood of terror – except somehow (as Kogan noted) we always forget. In *if*...., real terror is glimpsed this solitary time, during a revenge we probably applaud. Is this the reason we forget: that we project our grown-up war-maps back onto these bitter battles for the formation of the self – and in the process, mix up the real and the game? Yelling with hate, Travis rams the bayonet home.

Jaw Jaw

'I take this seriously' – a superbly fatuous remark to cut to from the yell and the stab, the satire exact. 'It's a quite blameless form of existentialism': with every word, the headmaster reveals his *un*seriousness. 'So often have I noticed that it's the *hair rebels* who step into the breach when there's a crisis.' His complacency is seamless, but there's a historical basis to its assumptions: 'You are too *intelligent* to be rebels.' In its Heroic Age, the EPS non-conformists were essential to the system – rogue energy was generated to a purpose. Expelled, Willoughby Cotton, schoolboy general of Rugby's Great Mutiny, afterwards headed the Bengal division of the British army, becoming

We are all meat

Commander-in-Chief in Bombay. He's almost the first genuine historical figure that Flashman meets – Fraser's point being that the buttoned-down anti-fun hegemony was only ever half the story.[76] The EPS people who made and ran the Empire in its greatness were its pranksters, its chancers, its cads – the fellows who like to blow stuff up.

Apologists

The headmaster pulls out a long drawer, and here's the chaplain, sitting up to accept the handshakes of the trio. Then he lies back down and the drawer is once more pushed closed. For pure Buñuelian daftness, this moment is unforgettable, anti-realist, dreamlike, unreadable within any clash of *moral* schemas. If villains sit back up, undead, it can't be a crime to kill them. Indeed, why even bother? Eternal return – already hinted at by Peanuts, with his other galaxies where they speak English – makes a nonsense of the headmaster's lecture *and* Travis's rebellion.

Here the rebels are in the well-appointed official heart of the beast, facing their topmost foe, but they just shake meek hands with their tormentors: the rules of the game don't allow you to escape the game. 'Work, play, *but don't mix the two*!' as Mr Kemp advised newcomers in the first chapter. Travis could sell himself as the new Willoughby Cotton – precisely the special rebel product all these overt and covert wargames and sexgames were designed to make of a child. Equals be co-opted equals fail.

Community Service†

They're not flogged, they're not fined. Instead, they have to clear the junk out from the lumber rooms, clambering down beneath the

The detritus of history

speechday stage into the school's forgotten spaces, where they find piled the detritus of its history. In *Stalky*, the trio climb round in the interstices of a school building, to push the corpse of a farm cat out under the floorboards of a rival house – as she decays, she starts to 'whisper to 'em in their dreams'.[77] Here the outsider element, in a far more radical breach of the psychic geometry of the school story, is living and vivid and attractive: the girl. Old rules no longer apply: hauling out and burning the hoarded rubbish, only to discover a vast cache of live weaponry, the full revolutionary army, all five at last assembled, can break entirely with the story's canonic frame. Any hope-filled engagement with documentary reality ends here, with flight into dreamtime.

A Foetus in Formalin†

A chaplain in a drawer, an alligator on a bonfire – in the third instance of undiluted Buñuelian surrealism, Travis wordlessly hands the girl a still-born baby in a pickle jar.

When this scene was being filmed, a technician (unnamed) stormed up to Sherwin: 'It has to be a sick mind to think up something like this. Really sick ... ' Anderson (reports Robinson) silenced his crew member brusquely, then patronised his pet screenwriter: 'Don't you see, you're facing them at one and the same time with the two things they fear most – birth and death? Of course they can't face up to it. I warned you they'd carry on like that. I don't see why you're surprised. That's what the film is about ...'[78]

So who is *they*? Everyone except Anderson? What the classroom calls 'thinking' can't address the power games in the hallway, let alone the bedroom, can't dissect the hierarchy affirmed by every exchange between master and slave, or rank and file. Because the Madras System legislates what passes for official knowledge within College, the school cannot begin to teach the analysis of the histories of its own structures of abuse – no self-knowledge, no wisdom – though that history lesson (once we paid close enough attention) did offer agonising, ambiguous hints, of mutual betrayal, of refusal to connect. And then there's the question of Anderson's own lapses of self-knowledge, of his (school-cultured?) will to bully and play mindgames.

Freezing scene after scene into perverse Barthesian syntagms drags up all sorts of hints, worries and problems from below the staged flow of the film. Seizing on this most minor of film genres, the classic English school-story form, Anderson worked into it a jostling subliminal tumult of poster images, slogans, grace notes of literary reference, romantic conventions and clichés, music, movement, noise and look. As he himself insisted, director and screenwriter, working on *Crusaders* together in the spring of 1967, went to view Vigo's *Zéro de conduite*: 'not for its anarchistic spirit – we had plenty of our own – [but for] Vigo's poetic method, episodic, fragmentary, charged'.[79] Where the canonic school story prior to *if....* had occluded all useable history of the EPS, in fact and myth, by formalising both, Anderson reorganises these meanings, first via sex and violence, film's primary codes, then via the poetry, fragmentation, watchful observation and reflective undercurrent he absorbed from such precursors as Vigo and Jennings.

In this scene all the darts are in flight; we are suspended between the end of games and the dawn of violent chaos. So many intricate systems of power have now been mapped – power transmitted in this sub-world via faith, discipline, the stones and the law; in classroom scenes, chapel scenes, sporting scenes, little ethnologies of local slang and hierarchy and comportment and coupledom; the bondage-form traceries of Gothic creativity; attitudes to wonder, pleasure, diversion and revelation; the dynamics of freedom and constraint, of acts and deserts, of passion and honour; the dialectics of fantasy, ferocity, affection, universality, tenderness ... How can the clash of so many systems of wisdom and perspective be represented, except confusingly? Conceding the complexity of this film's ambition (in order to declare its failure), Pauline Kael called Anderson a scourge, not a poet: always intelligent, impatient, didactic, scornful, what the director risked doing – with his press-release explanations and his bully-words ('poetry', 'intuition', 'commitment', 'repression', 'middleclass') – was to shut any remnant of Jute-like

Wisdoms in unreadable collision

openness down, to scorn hope, to explain, to justify, to close, to end: 'I don't see why you're surprised ...'

So what *does* the foetus mean? That official systems of knowledge and power are barren? That the still-born progeny of the techno-rational establishment is hideous and grotesque – or weirdly compelling, and beautiful? That rebels must accept they can't also belong to normal, happy, child-bearing families? That revolutionaries are a kind of doomed lab freak? That freedom is a space where women can survive only if they ostracise themselves from their nature? That terrorism – the radical individualist-moralist politics of pop spectacle – is a dead end? That in a Victorian museum-ruin like this, this rambling theatre of emotional concealment, someone might well store a pickled baby in a cupboard under a stage and forget about it? Or just nothing, nothing at all. Maybe all critical theory *is* just an alligator on a bonfire.

Theatre of War

Flanked by Latin-speaking knights in armour, as well as boys, teachers, parents and notables, the old boy giving the speech on Founder's Day, a military booby, talks rot: symbolism and *mise en scène* merge, ritual as moribund exclusionary jargon, a historically dishonest repository of pointless scholarship.[80] 'If the public schools had not existed,' raged Eric Rhode, 'Anderson would have had to create something like them, a barbarous world of clans and tyrannies ... It seems that [Anderson and Sherwin] look back yearningly to the Crusades and the Wars of the Roses – to times when, apparently, conflicts were simple and feelings plain.'[81]

Perhaps you glimpsed Jute that one last time, freckled chorister face catching the light as the mote breaks discipline to turn and gaze, but our put-upon little Justine is vanished back into the unrescued Brownian flow of boys – '*Men* of College', General Denson just addressed them, pompously, forlornly – as they flood from the severed stone arteries, to a stock swirl of organ. Jute never gets to be manly; he never gets to choose, or to judge. Meanwhile high in the flies – the gnarled turrets and spires of the symbolic fantasticality of this stagiest of official architectures – the rebel band look down into the quadrangle as so much Tudor theatre-in-the-round. The audience – we? – flee the interrupted speech and stage-smoke – into a second play space. The *Zeitgeist* triumphant in 1968 was a vast cultural stage invasion – the spectacle seized, the play made real, the pupils now the teachers. We know to mock all mumblers of Latin, but what happens when our beloved outlaws are also trapped acting out their part – knights errant, lonesome cowboys, urban guerrillas – in the intended wargames of their foes, their teacher-makers? Soon we will be under unambiguous attack; soon the gun will point *our* way. Real blood? Or is this just an impoverished realness, expelling everything the Whips of cinema class as uncool, and mowing it down as it flees?

'Bastards! Bastards!'
(Or 'It's the Yell that Counts!'): an elderly woman totes a Bren-gun, shrieking abuse, the anti-repression tantrums of AYM-ist orthodoxy calling up their own mad reflections. 'My God! We're on fire!' panics plain-speaking General Denson, the last to see what's going on, now reduced to comical statements of the obvious. Anderson disliked British film humour – too 'middleclass', of course[82] – but the scenes leading up to the climax deliver classic *Carry On* material: rote stuffiness in a crisis of its own making, deflated by the inadequacy of its responses. Yet the layers and fragments in 'Crusaders', the film's final chapter, are harder even to read than those in 'Ritual and Romance'.

As we enjoy the gunning down of pedants, fakes, robots, duffers and dupes – not to mention little old ladies, faces meanly filmed to look ugly, sterile, desperate – here's Christine Noonan electrifying in full battledress, with weapon. *A girl, a gun: cinema* – when 'manliness' meant every different, unVictorian thing from Arthur Lowe's podgy, deluded warrior Captain Mainwaring to McDowell as Jagger-droog Alex in *A Clockwork Orange* (1971), already there gathered an idolised band of radical new *womanliness*: Bernadine Dohrn, Leila Khaled, Astrid Proll ... In 1969, three New York members of the Weather Underground – two men and a woman – will smithereen themselves with their own bomb, and all hippy militancy with them. In the Stonewall uprising a mob of angry

A girl, a gun (right: Leila Khaled) ...

... cinema

transvestites will rout the cops. (In 1974, Anderson was planning a documentary about Baader-Meinhof.)

'They came up with a really stupid meaning.' What if we made everywhere the hallway and it turned out an even worse schoolroom? When the subjects of history step up on-stage, as masque not deed, the mask may be on the wrong face: the wretched and the lost remain outside, oiks and tarts still, valets and serfs and patsies, ignored and sidelined by the narcissism of the terrorist. Noonan is less the Girl-as-Undeluded-Outsider, objective Brechtian agent without a stake in this narrow sub-world, than exact, self-pleased, zipless reflection, tigergrowling in the café, of McDowell. Yes, the vision is iconic and prescient, but did we escape the metaphor yet? As the Travises – the Stalkies, the Baader-Meinhofs – despoil, College stands back, looks on: it wound the key; later it will explain the mess away. Yes, the rebel five are as sexy as Robin Hood, as a rock band, as an army of lovers – but being sexy doesn't make you right. Is there *any* lesson more urgent to be learnt from the 60s?

A Last Appeal to Reason

Moving slowly, the girl – hesitant or just deliberate? – takes her pistol from her belt and shoots the headmaster in the forehead. As an evident success on the world's terms, *if....* became a failure on its own. It fitted the temper of the times – and the times did its thinking for it. It meant to ask radical questions; it seemed to present world-historical solutions. But the Vietcong's anti-colonial revolution wasn't just a teenage hissy fit, still less an attention-seeking demand that the West – the 'grown-ups' – prove they cared by grabbing back control.

If You Can Keep Your Head ...

When Tom Brown is sent off to Rugby, his mother weeps and worries – he's sad too, but is consoled: his mettle is now to be tested. Thus, no doubt, many parents who send their sons away to boarding school, even those who liked and agreed with *if*.... Whence the amnesia? This is the mystery Frank Kogan cut into, in his report on Columbine: the facts immured in the heart of the school story; the pickled baby hidden under the dais. Real terror and real division are translated back into the stage furniture of the practice crusade, the grail-game it is imagined you will look back at and recall fondly. Meanwhile, what you learned battling your play foes, society will use – in you – battling against *its* enemies, *its* outsiders. Your ordeal – your play battles, your real pain – become the fables to lure and soothe those who come after. Destructiveness – self-destructiveness most of all – is just another leisure-industry body-gag, a very common one in 1968: *if*.... simply stalls, in a tremendous chaotic shell-burst of them.[83]

How Films End

Vigo's schoolboys made fun of their prison-guard teachers, before hopping off across the rooftops, mooning us beneath their trousers. As barbarians swarm over Cheltenham's spiked gables, as mortars blow holes in the lawns, what was implicit in the noises over *if*....'s opening credits is finally realised – the rage that simmers beneath slapstick: St Trinians with live ammunition and real death.

The sour anti-Hollywood ending was a late 60s cliché: as Pauline Kael (reviewing *Zabriskie Point* in 1969) wrote, 'Much of the hopelessness in movies like *if*.... and *Easy Rider* and *Medium Cool* and the new thrillers that kill off their protagonists is probably dictated not by a consideration of actual alternatives and the conclusion that there's no hope but simply by what seems daring and new and photogenic.'[84] In 1967, likeable antiheroes Bonnie and Clyde are thrust shuddering into a

Like St Trinians (*The Belles of St Trinians*, British Lion Film Corporation, 1954), but with live ammunition and real death

killing hail of bullets; in 1969, likeable antiheroes Butch Cassidy and the Sundance Kid escape *their* hail of bullets – which only hit after the film ends – and step into deathless, sepia-tone, freeze-frame mythology. 'Unhappy the film that needs heroes,' as Brecht might have said.

Could Anderson have known *if....* would be so in step with the industry *Zeitgeist*? Kael's point seems unfair: besides, the 'photogenic' climax is doggedly low budget, anti-realistic, *Dad's Army*-ish. But where Knightly's mother's cancer pierced you – 'What is necessary now is to be CONCRETE' – these last scenes instead pander to two more conventional needs: the director's for a climax, and ours for a message.

The raw freeze-frame finishing *Les Quatre cents coups* – which arguably re-instated the still in mainstream film grammar – leaves that movie unclosed, as if Truffaut had plonked one of Vigo's *Zéro*-kids on the beach the following day, and asked what next? How *should* films end? Reviewing *if....* for *Screen*, David Spiers (who liked it) had concluded: 'The fascist implications of the theme of the film are made even more disturbing coming as they do from somebody who has always aligned himself with the left.'[85] As Sherwin himself said on set, to David Robinson: 'This is what society does to good people and people who want to be free. This is what happens to Mick. He becomes as evil and as terrible as the headmaster or the general.'[86] School-as-metaphor is also always a soothing: because the identity given the hated Establishment in the end absolves *you*: 'Evil people like ... ourselves? Do you disagree?'

Endings are always also arguments about what constitutes an ending; what an ending – the most misleading element in all art – *does* ... Studied at leisure – when a scene's detail makes you smile and think; the history lesson, say, or even the flogging – then yes, all the layers of contradiction *can* be unpacked. (In 2002, Sherwin – favourite pupil finally shaking off master's glamour – described Anderson as the 'most un-Brechtian director I've ever met'.)[87] But in a season when genuinely alienated assassins were using real bullets, when actual imperialist invaders were dropping real bombs, the terrified swirl of these final scenes allow no such space. The shape of the tale demands a big bang, chaos and close: yet Anderson still also needs us to read carefully and closely, to connect and detect: to note and interpret the mirror-comparisons and polarities and references as they flash by; angry, armed crone versus supercool, armed babe; boy and girl rebels dressed up as Polish Resistance fighters; perfect mirrored compadres as revolutionary equals. Until here's Travis suddenly firing out at *us*, like the cowboy at the end of Edwin S. Porter's *The Great Train Robbery*, all the way back in

Neither manliness nor
beastliness

1903. Are we meant to be thinking of the massed firepower of the law, just out of frame? A moment before a Butch and Sundance semi-closure, two moments before a Bonnie and Clyde full stop, the judder of Travis's gun makes an inelegant, unsettling, ugly puppet of him, in close-up. Our final impression: his face, in a rictus of despair and failure.

How Books End

Anderson found few enough companions over the years, to share a life or make a work with – Sherwin, McDowell, a handful of others. To acknowledge the revolt could succeed, one of the prisoners at least has to cross the battle lines, to clamber up on stage and join them – Mrs Kemp, Biles, just one ugly old mother in a bad hat ... But the possibility of the triumph of the lovely band of the good is walled off behind the director's ruthless scepticism toward hope, change, heartsease. School may be a system to keep you in your 'proper' place, but even so certain teachers may help you set yourself free. This film seems to demand we fight for a better dialectic between teacher and taught: yet it ends up trapped – at the conscious level – by a refusal to be deluded by desire; by Anderson's disabling fear of sentimentality. In fact McDowell has said that the days making *if....* were the happiest of Anderson's life. So ask yourself: has any of *McDowell's* Anderson-less work since really been as good (let alone David Wood's or Christine Noonan's)?

To guarantee his integrity, Anderson chose isolation. Aggressively drawn to the castigation of the world as it is, he too easily found reasons for never addressing his own solitude – even though it's his sensitivity to solitude that redeems his best projects. As a political storyteller, he was sometimes bullying and dogmatic: as a documentarist, he was watchful, sensitive, still and intuitive. He was a stubborn, clever man who made films as much by instinct as reason, and this is the good *and* the bad of them. He never lost faith in the ability of the trapped to find or make their own truth: and this release – as he never quite admitted – was *collective*, the communal energy of gargoyle detail contained in the whole, the unity creative social chemistries at work below the level of consciousness. For film – like life – is mass work, not individual, and after the 60s, all art – for good or ill – belonged as much to its audience: this was the real cultural overturning, the power and the flaw of that decade. Instead of helping him, the convulsion iconified in the upheavals of 1968 – the audience stage invasion *as the work itself* – imprisoned him: to read Mick as choiceless, as the end seems to, is to rubber-stamp forever Anderson's belief that the connection he craved would exile him from his own gifts. The comfortable, nostalgic response to *if....* can make a reactionary film of it – but all that means is that we're still trying too hard to lock the confusion down into a nice safe focus-group moral. 'However smart they were,' writes Kogan, 'they did not look inside themselves because looking at whatever was closing them off would have hurt too much.' Terrorism is a catastrophe as politics, *at best* an act of suicidal, selfish despair: did Anderson want his audiences to embrace and approve it, or trust them to see through it? 'Some people cannot be trusted with a helpless body,' writes Califia. So shouldn't Anderson have seen what was coming to schools, to Dunblane, to Columbine? *But he did.* Perhaps he didn't ask hard enough questions – but of course (thinking of Brecht to the end) this part is *our* job ...

To be a man, my son, you must be unlike all the conformists round about you, wrote Kipling: but if a moral life can only be a solitary life, yes, the tormented rebel will always end up gunning down his own – as he gazes desperately out at us, longing for our love. A form of existentialism which is *never* considered blameless. In the end, *if....* is about something far more deeply taboo than Establishment stupidity or dissident sex or the destructive anarchist spark, than nightly buggery and beatings or classical construes or even compulsory rugby. Neither the manliness of the rebel nor the beastliness of the spree-killer – but loneliness. Not loneliness as explanation or excuse, but loneliness as tetchily, tenderly documented learning ground of all. Return to his roots, to blow them up – and walk away?

'In the end,' says Anderson, 'the artist is on his own.'[88]

APPENDIX: LINDSAY ANDERSON AND FREE CINEMA
. . . .

The main statement of intent was signed by Lindsay Anderson, Tony Richardson, Karol Reisz and Lorenza Mazzetti:

> *As film-makers we believe that*
> *No film can be too personal.*
> *The image speaks. Sound amplifies and comments. Size is irrelevant.*
> *Perfection is not an aim.*
> *An attitude means a style. A style means an attitude.*

A second manifesto was signed by Anderson alone:

> *With a 16mm camera, and minimal resources, you cannot achieve very much – in*
> *commercial terms. You cannot make a feature film, and your possibilities of*
> *experiment are severely restricted. But you can use your eyes and ears. You can*
> *give indications. You can make poetry.*

Though Anderson's documentaries began back in 1948 with *Meet the Pioneers*, a half-hour promotional short about Yorkshire manufacturers Sutcliffe Co., the first to be included in 'Free Cinema' (as defined in 1956) was *Wakefield Express* (1952), a half-hour portrait of a local community's image of itself, via its ceremonies, music and newspaper, which played in in the third 'Free Cinema' programme, in 1957. *Every Day Except Christmas* (1957), about the Covent Garden market, headed this third programme, rubric 'Look at Britain', and won Venice Grand Prix for Best Documentary. *O Dreamland* (1953) headed the first programme, as discussed in the main text (Anderson also edited Lorenza Mazzetti's *Together*, about two deaf-mute East End dock-workers). Though it won the 1954 Oscar for Best Short Subject, *Thursday's Child*, co-directed by Guy Brenton about deaf-mute children, did not appear in a 'Free Cinema' programme – Anderson rather disliked it.

   In 1986, Anderson blithely redefined 'Free Cinema' to sum up a very complicated three-decade legacy, expanding it into an umbrella term for every film he, Reisz and Richardson would go on to make in England – at least until the other two escaped to Hollywood. Other names were always problematic. 'British New Wave' merely hung itself on French coat-tails; 'Kitchen Sink Drama' was snide, always disliked by insiders; 'Angry Young Men' likewise, and besides, some AYM-ers were by the mid-80s very blimpish indeed, their thirty-year-old triumph become a self-important bore. But 'Free Cinema', this brief, semi-forgotten movement named and shaped by Anderson himself, had *not* been spoiled by its success. The occasion of the redefinition was a half-hour television polemic in LWT's *British Cinema: Personal View* series, Anderson's *Free Cinema 1956–?* a retort to producer David Puttnam's claim – in *Marxism Today*, apparently, while promoting 'British Film Year' – that no indigenous cinema style had ever existed in the UK. The point of the reinvention – which expanded 'Free Cinema' to encompass *if....* above all – was to rescue ideals and intentions from the spite of fashion and the wreck of facts.

NOTES

· ·

1 Frank Kogan, 'School's Been Blown to Pieces', *Village Voice*, 28 April– 4 May 1999. This article and related interviews can be found at www.villagevoice.com/issues/9917/kogan. php,…/kogan2.php and …/kogan3.php

2 Ibid.

3 Lindsay Anderson, 'Notes for a Preface', Lindsay Anderson and David Sherwin, *if….* (London: Lorrimer, 1969), p. 10.

4 Stuart Turnbull in *Sleazenation*; David Stubbs in *Uncut*; James Mottram in *What's on in London*. All from 2002: see http://www.bfi. org.uk/collections/release/if/critics.html

5 David Sherwin, *Going Mad in Hollywood– and Life with Lindsay Anderson* (Harmondsworth: Penguin, 1996), p. 2.

6 It's hard to believe that potential producers weren't being selected by Sherwin and Howlett for their unsuitability. Sherwin, *Going Mad*, pp. 2–4; Gavin Lambert, *Mainly about Lindsay Anderson: A Memoir* (London: Faber & Faber, 2000), p. 138.

7 Except where stated, anecdotes about the making of *if….* come from Sherwin, *Going Mad*, and Lambert, *Mainly about Lindsay Anderson*.

8 Lindsay Anderson, *British Cinema: A Personal View: Free Cinema 1956–?* (LWT broadcast, 19 March 1986).

9 Lindsay Anderson, 'Only Connect: Some Aspects of the Work of Humphrey Jennings', *Sight and Sound* vol. 23 no. 4, Spring 1954, reprinted in Brian Winston, *Fires Were Started–* (London: BFI, 1999), pp. 70–5.

10 Anderson, *British Cinema: A Personal View*.

11 Lindsay Anderson, 'Get Out and Push', quoted in Gavin Lambert, *Mainly about*, p. 73; originally collected in Tom Maschler (ed.), *Declaration* (London: MacGibbon & Kee, 1957).

12 The intended project was a portmanteau film, with two other Delaney-scripted shorts, directed by Tony Richardson and Peter Brook, but plans kept changing, the other shorts weren't made and *The White Bus* never had full release.

13 Sherwin, *Going Mad*, p. 14.

14 Lambert, *Mainly about*, p. 139.

15 David Gladwell, 'Editing Anderson's *if….*', *Screen* vol. 10 no. 1, January–February 1969, p. 25.

16 Or possibly Sherwin's. Lambert, *Mainly about*, p. 141.

17 An invaluable resource for *if….*-related interviews and material is Alex D. Thrawn's website www.malcolmmcdowell.net

18 David Robinson, *Sight and Sound* vol. 37 no. 3, Summer 1968, pp. 130–1; David Robinson, 'Lindsay Anderson's Schooldays', *Times*, 2 April 1968.

19 Gladwell, 'Editing Anderson's *if….*', pp. 24–5.

20 Robinson, *Sight and Sound*, pp. 130–1.

21 The Eady quota required that a given proportion of films shown in British cinemas in any one year had to be British.

22 Eric Rhode, 'Life in Britain', *Listener*, 26 December 1968.

23 Pauline Kael, 'School Days, School Days', *New Yorker*, 15 March 1969, collected in Pauline Kael, *Going Steady: Film Writings 1968–1969* (New York/London: Marion Boyars, 1994), pp. 279–86.

24 Gavin Millar, *Sight and Sound* vol. 38 no. 1, Winter 68–9, pp. 42–3.

25 Anderson, 'Notes for a Preface', p. 9.

26 Proverbs 4:7 was a favourite of Anderson's and also features in *The White Bus*.

27 Rudyard Kipling, 'In Ambush', *Stalky and Co* (1899; Oxford: Oxford University Press, 1987), p. 37.

28 Rudyard Kipling, 'Brother Square-Toes', *Rewards and Fairies* (1910; London: Piccolo, 1975), p. 144.

29 Gladwell, 'Editing Anderson's *if….*', p. 31.

30 Frank Kogan, 'Democratising the Intellect', in Tom Carson, Kit Rachlis and Jeff Salamon (eds), *Don't Stop 'til You Get Enough: Essays in Honor of Robert Christgau* (Austin, TX: Nortex Press limited edition, 2002), available via www.robertchristgau.com/pp/bk-fest.php. A revised version, 'The Presentation of Self in Everyday Life', will be published in Frank Kogan, *Real Punks Don't Wear Black* (Athens and London: University of Georgia Press, due 2005).

31 'Six Characters in Search of Auteurs: A Discussion about the French Cinema', *Cahiers du Cinéma* no. 71, May 1957, collected in Jim Hillier (ed.), *Cahiers du Cinéma: The 1950s – Neo-Realism, Hollywood, New Wave* (Cambridge, MA: Harvard Film Studies, 1985), p. 32.
32 *Typically British*, directed Stephen Frears, BFI, 1994.
33 Jean-Luc Godard, 'La Photo du mois', collected in Hillier, *Cahiers*, p. 51.
34 See my 'Y is for Youth', *Sight and Sound* vol. 8 no. 5, June 1998.
35 Hippolyte Taine, *Notes on England* (London: Thames & Hudson, 1957), p. 109.
36 Rhode, 'Life in Britain'.
37 Lambert, *Mainly about*, p. 88
38 The term 'Whips' also maps British Parliamentary protocol onto the underworld of sexual sado-masochism, of course.
39 Lambert, *Mainly about*, p. 139.
40 Stephen Lowe, *Arthur Lowe: Dad's Memory* (London: Virgin Books, 1997), p. 87.
41 Sections whose subheads are marked † discuss scenes or sequences shot in black and white.
42 So says Lambert, *Mainly about*, pp. 12, 142.
43 Ibid., p. 89.
44 Thus the words on the plaque at Rugby School itself, telling the William Webb-Ellis legend. But the legend seems to have emerged only in the late nineteenth century: certainly no mention of it is found in *Tom Brown's Schooldays*.
45 Thomas Hughes, *Tom Brown's Schooldays, by An Old Boy* (1857; London: Macmillan and Co., 1892), p. 290.
46 George MacDonald Fraser, *Flashman in the Great Game* (1975; London: HarperCollins, 1999), p. 232.
47 Lambert, *Mainly about*, pp. 10, 57, 97–103.
48 Dan Rebellato, *1956 and All That: The Making of Modern British Drama* (London: Routledge, 1999), pp. 213–15.
49 Perhaps inevitably, the man in charge of the Wolfenden Commission was a former EPS headmaster: John Wolfenden, Shrewsbury School, 1947–50.

50 Anderson, *British Cinema: A Personal View*.
51 Anthony Page, quoted in Lambert, *Mainly about*, p. 93.
52 Ibid., p. 216.
53 The film was passed 'X' in the UK and the US. As well as Christine Noonan's pubic hair in the café scene, the British censors allowed a brief, unprecedented frontal shot of Mary MacLeod in the dormitories, but demanded substitute shots in the boys' shower scene, to excise the equivalent male view. In the US, where the classification system was voluntary, all male and MacLeod's pubes were omitted, so the film could be an 'A' outside New York (that is, an 'R': *Variety*, 21 May 1969). The film-makers demanded rear-view substitutions. Dialogue and actions containing sexual reference or implication were cut in Australia, Eire and South Africa. In Greece, the entire final sequence was cut. No one saw the film at all in Portugal. (See Anderson, 'Notes for a Preface', pp. 10–11.)
54 Lambert, *Mainly about*, pp. 54–5.
55 Anderson, 'Notes for a Preface', p. 9.
56 Anderson, 'Only Connect'.
57 All quotes in this paragraph from Anderson, 'Notes for a Preface', p. 10.
58 Here's Kael's accurate guess, for example: '... the results of accident and economy – I assume when the light wasn't adequate for using color film, they went on shooting with black and white': Kael, 'School Days, School Days', p. 284. Also intriguing: David Gladwell doesn't even mention this issue in 'Editing Anderson's *if....*'
59 Anderson, 'Notes for a Preface', p. 12.
60 Sherwin, *Going Mad*, pp. 20–1.
61 Sherwin quoted in 'The Scene in the Café', production notes, *if....* promotional pack, Paramount Press Office, 1968.
62 'Too Stark for Mr Chips', *Sunday Telegraph*, 15 December 1968.
63 Actor Richard Wallace died of AIDS in 1997.
64 Lambert, *Mainly about*, p. 142; Anderson and Sherwin, 'Notes for a Preface', p. 12.
65 Anderson to Bill Pertwee, *The Life of Arthur Lowe* radio documentary, quoted in Lowe, *Arthur Lowe*, p. 81.

66 Edwards came out in his 1984 memoirs, *Six of the Best*. Jimmy Edwards, *Six of the Best* (Robson Books, 1984).
67 Pat Califia, 'The Calyx of Isis', *Macho Sluts* (Boston: Alyson Publications, 1988), p. 115.
68 Califia, Introduction, *Macho Sluts*, p. 27.
69 Rebellato, *1956 and All That*, pp. 96–8.
70 Gladwell, 'Editing Anderson's *if....*', p. 31.
71 Sherwin, *Going Mad*, p. 19.
72 See Walter Benjamin, 'What Is Epic Theatre?', 1939, collected in Walter Benjamin, *Illuminations*, ed. Hannah Arendt (New York: Schocken Books, 1968), pp. 147–54.
73 Lambert, *Mainly about*, pp. 24–6.
74 Sherwin, *Going Mad*, p. 14.
75 *O Lucky Man!* (1973) and *Britannia Hospital* (1982) both starred Malcolm McDowell as a character named Mick Travis, as well as several other actors from *if....*. These and *if2*, a project halted by Anderson's death in 1994, all had scripts by David Sherwin.
76 George MacDonald Fraser, *Flashman* (1969; London: HarperCollins, 1999), pp. 90–1.
77 Kipling, 'An Unsavoury Interlude', *Stalky and Co*, p. 83.
78 Robinson, *Sight and Sound*, pp. 130–1.

Sherwin remembers the attack slightly differently, noting that the technician's wife had just had a miscarriage, see Sherwin, *Going Mad*, p. 23.
79 Lambert, *Mainly about*, p. 139.
80 Pointless like this perhaps: even Winchester, first of the Nine, wouldn't be founded for more than a century after the final crusade. Cheltenham College of course dates from 1841.
81 Rhode, 'Life in Britain'.
82 Anderson, *British Cinema: A Personal View*.
83 David Gladwell notes that the entire final sequence, cut together at speed for an early screening for Paramount, was subsequently left more or less unchanged. Gladwell, 'Editing Anderson's *if....*', p. 31.
84 Pauline Kael, 'The Beauty of Destruction', *New Yorker*, 21 February 1970, collected in Pauline Kael, *Deeper into Movies* (London: Calder and Boyars, 1975), p. 117.
85 David Spiers, *Screen* vol. 10 no. 2, March–April 1969, pp. 85–9.
86 Robinson, *Sight and Sound*, pp. 130–1.
87 Sherwin interviewed by Paul Sutton in *Camera 1*, 2002. The interview can be found at www.malcolmmcdowell.net
88 Lambert, *Mainly about*, p. 96.

CREDITS

. . . .

if....

United Kingdom/USA
1968

Directed by
Lindsay Anderson
Produced by
Michael Medwin,
Lindsay Anderson
Screenplay by
David Sherwin
From the original script by
David Sherwin, John Howlett
Director of Photography
Miroslav Ondricek
Editor
David Gladwell
Production Designed by
Jocelyn Herbert
**Music Composed and
Conducted by**
Marc Wilkinson

© Paramount Pictures
Corporation
Production Company
Made by Memorial Enterprises
Limited
[Executive Producer
Roy Baird]
Production Accountant
Brian Brockwell
Production Manager
Gavrik Losey
**Assistant to the
Producers**
Neville Thompson
[Production Secretary
Zelda Barron]
Assistant Director
John Stoneman
[2nd Assistant Director
Tim Van Rellim]
**Assistants to the
Director**
Stephen Frears
Stuart Baird
Continuity
Valerie Booth
Casting Director
Miriam Brickman

Cameraman
Chris Menges
Camera Operator
Brian Harris
Camera Assistant
Michael Seresin
Electrical Supervisor
Roy Larner
Electrical Contractors
Lee Electrics
[Explosions
Pat Moore]
Assistant Editors
Ian Rakoff
Michael Ellis
[Art Director
Brian Eatwell]
Construction Manager
Jack Carter
Wardrobe
Shura Cohen
Make-up
Betty Blattner
Soundtrack
Sanctus from 'Missa Luba'
(Philips Recording)
[performed by Les
Troubadours du Roi
Baudouin; Toccata from
'Symphonie pour orgue No. 5'
by Charles-Marie Widor]
Sound Recordist
Christian Wangler
Dubbing Mixer
Doug Turner
[Effects Mixer
David Maiden]
Dubbing Editor
Alan Bell
Transport
Jim Hughes
Production Processing
Humphries Laboratories
[Gymnastic Adviser
Sergeant Instructor Rushforth]
[Motorbike Assistance
Michael White,
Malcolm Miles]
[Interpreter
Jirina Tvarochova]

[Fight Choreography
Peter Brayham]

Cast
Crusaders
Malcolm McDowell
Michael 'Mick' Travis
David Wood
Johnny Knightly
Richard Warwick
Wallace
Christine Noonan
the girl
Rupert Webster
Bobby Philips

Whips
Robert Swann
Rowntree
Hugh Thomas
Richard Denson
Michael Cadman
Fortinbras
Peter Sproule
Barnes

Staff
Peter Jeffrey
headmaster
Anthony Nicholls
General Denson
Arthur Lowe
Mr Kemp
Mona Washbourne
matron
Mary MacLeod
Mrs Kemp
Geoffrey Chater
Reverend Woods, chaplain
Ben Aris
John Thomas
Graham Crowden
Mr Stewart, history master
Charles Lloyd Pack
classics master

Seniors
Guy Ross
Stephans
Robin Askwith

Keating
Richard Everett
Pussy Graves
Philip Bagenal
Peanuts
Nicholas Page
Cox
Robert Yetzes
Fisher
David Griffin
Willens
Graham Sharman
Van Eyssen
Richard Tombleson
Baird

Juniors
Richard Davis
Machin
Brian Pettifer
Biles
Michael Newport
Brunning
Charles Sturridge
Markland
Sean Bury
Jute
Martin Beaumont
Hunter

[uncredited]
John Garrie
music master, staff
Tommy Godfrey
school porter, staff
Ellis Dale
motorcycle salesman
Peter Jaques
schoolmaster
Simon Ward
schoolboy

10,021 feet
111 minutes 21 seconds

Locations
Cheltenham College;
Aldenham School;
Shepherds Bush, London

Credits compiled by
Markku Salmi

ALSO PUBLISHED

An Actor's Revenge
Ian Breakwell
Andrei Rublev
Robert Bird
L'Âge d'or
Paul Hammond
L'Année dernière à Marienbad
Jean-Louis Leutrat
Annie Hall
Peter Cowie
L'Atalante
Marina Warner
L'avventura
Geoffrey Nowell-Smith
Belle de Jour
Michael Wood
The Big Heat
Colin McArthur
The Big Sleep
David Thomson
The Birds
Camille Paglia
Blackmail
Tom Ryall
The Blue Angel
S. S. Prawer
Bonnie and Clyde
Lester D. Friedman
Boudu Saved from Drowning
Richard Boston
Bride of Frankenstein
Alberto Manguel
Brief Encounter
Richard Dyer
Das Cabinet des Dr. Caligari
David Robinson
Cat People
Kim Newman
Chinatown
Michael Eaton
Citizen Kane
Laura Mulvey
Double Indemnity
Richard Schickel
Les Enfants du paradis
Jill Forbes
42nd Street
J. Hoberman
"Fires Were Started – "
Brian Winston
The Ghost and Mrs Muir
Frieda Grafe
Greed
Jonathan Rosenbaum
Gun Crazy
Jim Kitses
High Noon
Phillip Drummond
I Know Where I'm Going!
Pam Cook
In a Lonely Place
Dana Polan
In the Realm of the Senses
Joan Mellen
It's a Gift
Simon Louvish
Ivan the Terrible
Yuri Tsivian
Kind Hearts and Coronets
Michael Newton
The Life and Death of Colonel Blimp
A. L. Kennedy
Lolita
Richard Corliss
M
Anton Kaes
The Magnificent Ambersons
V. F. Perkins
The Manchurian Candidate
Greil Marcus
A Matter of Life and Death
Ian Christie
Meet Me in St. Louis
Gerald Kaufman
Metropolis
Thomas Elsaesser
Mother India
Gayatri Chatterjee
Napoléon
Nelly Kaplan
The Night of the Hunter
Simon Callow
La Nuit américaine
Roger Crittenden
October
Richard Taylor
Odd Man Out
Dai Vaughan
Olympia
Taylor Downing
Palm Beach Story
John Pym
Pépé le Moko
Ginette Vincendeau
Performance
Colin MacCabe
Queen Christina
Marcia Landy & Amy Villarejo
Red River
Suzanne Liandrat-Guigues
Rio Bravo
Robin Wood
Rocco and His Brothers
Sam Rohdie
Rome Open City
David Forgacs
Sanshô Dayû
Dudley Andrew & Carole Cavanaugh
The Searchers
Edward Buscombe
Seven Samurai
Joan Mellen
The Seventh Seal
Melvyn Bragg
Shadows
Ray Carney
Shane
Edward Countryman & Evonne von Heussen-Countryman
Singin' in the Rain
Peter Wollen
Stagecoach
Edward Buscombe
Sunrise – A Song of Two Humans
Lucy Fischer
Taxi Driver
Amy Taubin
The Third Man
Rob White
Things to Come
Christopher Frayling
To Be or Not to Be
Peter Barnes
Vertigo
Charles Barr
Went the Day Well?
Penelope Houston
Wild Strawberries
Philip & Kersti French
The Wizard of Oz
Salman Rushdie

If you would like further information about future BFI Film Classics or about other books on film, media and popular culture from BFI Publishing, please write to:

BFI Film Classics
BFI Publishing
21 Stephen Street
London W1T 1LN

BFI Film Classics '... could scarcely be improved upon ... informative, intelligent, jargon-free companions.'
The Observer

Each book in the BFI Publishing Film Classics series honours a great film from the history of world cinema. With new titles published each year, the series is rapidly building into a collection representing some of the best writing on film. If you would like to receive further information about future Film Classics or about other books on film, media and popular culture from BFI Publishing, please fill in your name and address and return this card to the BFI.* (No stamp required if posted in the UK, Channel Islands, or Isle of Man.)

NAME

ADDRESS

POSTCODE

E-MAIL ADDRESS:

WHICH *BFI FILM CLASSIC* DID YOU BUY?

* In North America and Asia (except India), please return your card to:
University of California Press, Web Department, 2120 Berkeley Way, Berkeley, CA 94720, USA

**BFI Publishing
21 Stephen Street
FREEPOST 7
LONDON
W1E 4AN**